PARTNERS OF CHANCE

I0554542

HENRY HERBERT KNIBBS

1st WORLD
LIBRARY
Literary Society

Partners of Chance

Henry Herbert Knibbs

© 1st World Library, 2007
PO Box 2211
Fairfield, IA 52556
www.1stworldlibrary.com
First Edition

LCCN: 2007930899

Softcover ISBN: 978-1-4218-4874-7
Hardcover ISBN: 978-1-4218-4777-1
eBook ISBN: 978-1-4218-4971-3

Purchase *"Partners of Chance"*
as a traditional bound book at:
www.1stWorldLibrary.com/purchase.asp?ISBN=978-1-4218-4874-7

1st World Library is a literary, educational organization
dedicated to:

- Creating a free internet library of downloadable ebooks

- Hosting writing competitions and offering book publishing
scholarships.

Interested in more 1st World Library books? contact:
literacy@1stworldlibrary.com
Check us out at: www.1stworldlibrary.com

1st World Library Literary Society

Giving Back to the World

"If you want to work on the core problem, it's early school literacy."

- James Barksdale, former CEO of Netscape

"No skill is more crucial to the future of a child, or to a democratic and prosperous society, than literacy."

- Los Angeles Times

"Literacy... means far more than learning how to read and write... The aim is to transmit... knowledge and promote social participation."

- UNESCO

"Literacy is not a luxury, it is a right and a responsibility. If our world is to meet the challenges of the twenty-first century we must harness the energy and creativity of all our citizens."

- President Bill Clinton

"Parents should be encouraged to read to their children, and teachers should be equipped with all available techniques for teaching literacy, so the varying needs and capacities of individual kids can be taken into account."

- Hugh Mackay

CONTENTS

I. LITTLE JIM 7

II. PANHANDLE 13

III. A MINUTE TOO LATE 22

IV. "A LITTLE GREEN RIVER"..29

V. "TOP HAND ONCE"..36

VI. A HORSE-TRADE...50

VII. AT THE WATER-HOLE..63

VIII. HIGH HEELS AND MOCCASINS 72

IX. AT THE BOX-S 83

X. TO TRY HIM OUT 89

XI. PONY TRACKS...94

XII. JIMMY AND THE LUGER GUN 102

XIII. AT AUNT JANE'S... 110

XIV. ANOTHER GAME... 120

XV. MORE PONY TRACKS.. 137

XVI. SAN ANDREAS TOWN.. 143

XVII. THAT MESCAL 153

XVIII. JOE SCOTT 161

XIX. DORRY COMES TO TOWN...................................... 167

XX. ALONG THE FOOTHILLS 175

XXI. "GIT ALONG CAYUSE"... 189

XXII. BOX-S BUSINESS 196

XXIII. THE HOLE-IN-THE-WALL 203

XXIV. CHEYENNE PLAYS BIG... 209

XXV. TWO TRAILS HOME 216

CHAPTER I

LITTLE JIM

Little Jim knew that something strange had happened, because Big Jim, his father, had sold their few head of cattle, the work team, and the farm implements, keeping only the two saddle-horses and the pack-horse, Filaree. When Little Jim asked where his mother had gone, Big Jim told him that she had gone on a visit, and would be away a long time. Little Jim wanted to know if his mother would ever come back. When Big Jim said that she would not, Little Jim manfully suppressed his tears, and, being of that frontier stock that always has an eye to the main chance, he thrust out his hand. "Well, I'll stick with you, dad. I reckon we can make the grade."

Big Jim turned away and stood for a long time gazing out of the cabin window toward town. Presently he felt a tug at his coat-sleeve.

"Is ma gone to live in town?"

"Yes."

"Then why don't you go get her?"

"She don't want to come back, Jimmy."

Little Jim could not understand this. Yet he had often heard his mother complain of their life on the homestead, and as often he had watched his father sitting grimly at table, saying nothing in reply to his wife's querulous complainings. The boy knew that his father had worked hard to make a home. They had all worked hard. But, then, that had seemed the only thing to do.

Presently Big Jim swung round as though he had made a decision. He lighted the lamp in the kitchen and made a fire. Little Jim scurried out to the well with a bucket. Little Jim was a hustler, never waiting to be told what to do. His mother was gone. He did not know why. But he knew that folks had to eat and sleep and work. While his father prepared supper, Little Jim rolled up his own shirt-sleeves and washed vigorously. Then he filled the two glasses on the table, laid the plates and knives and forks, and finding nothing else to do in the house, just then, he scurried out again and returned with his small arms filled with firewood.

Big Jim glanced at him. "I guess we don't need any more wood, Jimmy. We'll be leaving in the morning."

"What? Leavin' here?"

His father nodded.

"Goin' to town, dad?"

"No. South."

"Just us two, all alone?"

"Yes. Don't you want to go?"

Henry Herbert Knibbs

"Sure! But I wish ma was comin', too."

Big Jim winced. "So do I, Jimmy. But I guess we can get along all right. How would you like to visit Aunt Jane, down in Arizona?"

"Where them horn toads and stingin' lizards are?"

"Yes—and Gila monsters and all kinds of critters."

"Gee! Has Aunt Jane got any of 'em on her ranch?"

Big Jim forced a smile. "I reckon so."

Little Jim's face was eager. "Then I say, let's go. Mebby I can get to shoot one. Huntin' is more fun than workin' all the time. I guess ma got tired of workin', too. She said that was all she ever expected to do, 'long as we lived out here on the ranch. But she never told *me* she was goin' to quit."

"She didn't tell me, either, Jimmy. But you wouldn't understand."

Jimmy puckered his forehead. "I guess ma kind of throwed us down, didn't she, dad?"

"We'll have to forget about it," said Big Jim slowly. "Down at Aunt Jane's place in—"

"Somethin' 's burnin', dad!"

Big Jim turned to the stove. Little Jim gazed at his father's back critically. There was something in the stoop of the broad shoulders that was unnatural, strange—something that caused Little Jim to hesitate in his questioning. Little Jim idolized his father, and, with unfailing intuition, believed in him to the last word. As for his mother, who had left without explanation and would never return—Little Jim missed her, but more through habit of association than with actual grief.

He knew that his mother and father had not gotten along very well for some time. And now Little Jim recalled something that his mother had said: "He's as much your boy as he is mine, Jim Hastings, and, if you are set on sending him to school, for goodness' sake get him some decent clothes, which is more than I have had for many a year."

Until then Jimmy had not realized that his clothing or his mother's was other than it should be. Moreover, he did not want to go to school. He preferred to work on the ranch with his father. But it was chiefly the tone of his mother's voice that had impressed him. For the first time in his young life, Little Jim felt that he was to blame for something which he could not understand. He was accustomed to his mother's sudden fits of unreasonable anger, often followed by a cuff, or sharp reprimand. But she had never mentioned his need of better clothing before, nor her own need.

As for being as much his father's boy as his mother's—Little Jim felt that he quite agreed to that, and, if anything, that he belonged more to his father, who was kind to him, than to any one else in the world. Little Jim, trying to reason it out, now thought that he knew why his mother had left home. She had gone to live in town that she might have better clothes and be with folks and not wear her fingers to the bone simply for a bed and three meals a day, as Little Jim had heard her say more than once.

But the trip to Aunt Jane's, down in Arizona, was too vivid in his imagination to allow room for pondering. Big Jim had said they were to leave in the morning. So, while supper was cooking, Little Jim slipped into his bedroom and busied himself packing his own scant belongings. Presently his father called him. Little Jim plodded out bearing his few spare clothes corded in a neat bundle, with an old piece of canvas for the covering. His father had taught him to pack.

Big Jim stared. Then a peculiar expression flitted across his face. Little Jim was always for the main chance.

"I'm all hooked up to hit the trail, dad."

In his small blue overalls and jumper, in his alert and manful attitude, Little Jim was a pocket edition of his father.

"Where's your shootin'-iron?" queried Big Jim jokingly.

"Why, she's standin' in the corner, aside of yours. A man don't pack his shootin'-iron in his bed-roll when he hits the trail. He keeps her handy."

"For stingin' lizards, eh?"

"For 'most anything. Stingin' lizards, Injuns, or hoss-thieves, or anything that we kin shoot. We ain't takin' no chances on this here trip."

Big Jim gestured toward the table and pulled up his chair. Little Jim was too heartily interested in the meal to notice that his father gazed curiously at him from time to time. Until then, Big Jim had thought of his small son as a chipper, sturdy, willing boy—his boy. But now, Little Jim seemed suddenly to have become an actual companion, a partner, a sharer in things as they were and were to be.

Hard work and inherent industry had developed in Little Jim an independence that would have been considered precocious in the East. Big Jim was glad that the mother's absence did not seem to affect the boy much. Little Jim seemed quite philosophical about it. Yet, deep in his heart, Little Jim missed his mother, more than his father realized. The house seemed strangely empty and quiet. And it had seemed queer that Big Jim should cook the supper, and, later, wash the dishes.

That evening, just before they went to bed, Big Jim ransacked the bureau, sorting out his own things, and laying aside a few things that his wife had left: a faded pink ribbon, an old pair of high-heeled slippers, a torn and unmended apron, and an old gingham dress. Gathering these things together, Big Jim stuffed them in the kitchen stove. Little Jim watched him silently.

But when his father came from the stove and sat down, Little Jim slipped over to him. "Dad, are you mad at ma for leavin' us?" he queried.

Big Jim shook his head. "No, Jimmy. Just didn't want to leave her things around, after we had gone. Benson'll be movin' in sometime this week. I sold our place to him."

"The stove and beds and everything?"

"Everything."

Little Jim wrinkled his nose and sniffed. "Them things you put in the stove smell just like brandin' a critter," he said, gesturing toward the kitchen.

Big Jim gazed hard at his young son. Then he smiled to himself, and shook his head. "Just like brandin' a critter," he repeated, half to himself. "Just like brandin' a critter."

Henry Herbert Knibbs

CHAPTER II

PANHANDLE

While his friends and neighbors called Jim Hastings "Big Jim," he was no more than average size—compact, vigorous, reared in the Wyoming cattle lands, and typical of the country. He was called Big Jim simply to distinguish him from Little Jim, who was as well known in Laramie as his father. Little Jim, when but five years of age, rode his own pony, jogging alongside his father when they went to town, where he was decidedly popular with the townsfolk because of his sturdy independence and humorous grin.

Little Jim talked horses and cattle and ranching with the grown-ups and took their good-natured joshing philosophically. He seldom retorted hastily, but, rather, blinked his eyes and wrinkled his forehead as he digested this or that pleasantry, and either gave it the indifferent acknowledgment of "Shucks! Think you can josh *me*?" or, if the occasion and the remark seemed to call for more serious consideration, he rose to it manfully, and often to the embarrassment of the initial speaker.

Little Jim liked to go to town with his father, yet he considered town really a sort of suburb to his real world, the homestead, which he had seen change from a prairie level of unfenced space to a small—and to him—complete kingdom of pasture lot, hayfield, garden, corrals, stable, and house. Town was simply a place to which you went to buy things, get the mail, exchange views on the weather and grazing, and occasionally help the hands load a shipment of cattle. Little Jim helped by sitting on the top rail of the pens and commenting on the individual characteristics of the cattle, and, sometimes, of the men loading them. In such instances he found opportunity to pay off old scores. Incidentally he kept the men in good humor by his lively comment.

Little Jim was six years of age when his mother left to resume her former occupation of waitress in the station restaurant of Laramie, where she had been popular because of her golden hair, her blue eyes, and her ability to "talk back" to the regular customers in a manner which they seemed to enjoy. Big Jim married her when he was not much more than a boy—twenty, in fact; and during the first few years they were happy together. But homesteading failed to supply more than their immediate needs.

Occasional trips to town at first satisfied the wife's craving for the attention and admiration that most men paid to her rather superficial good looks. But as the years slipped by, with no promise of easier conditions, she became dissatisfied, shrewish, and ashamed of her lack of pretty things to wear. Little Jim was, of course, as blind to all this as he was to his need for anything other than his overalls, shoes, and jumper. He thought his mother was pretty and he often told her so.

Meanwhile, Big Jim tried to blind himself to his wife's growing dissatisfaction. He was too much of a man to argue her own short-comings as against his inability to do more for her than he was doing. But when she did leave, with simply a brief note saying that she was tired of it all, and would take care of herself, what hit Big Jim the hardest was the fact that she could give up Little Jim without so much as a word about him. Every one liked Little Jim, and the mother's going proved something that Big Jim had tried to ignore for several years—that his wife cared actually nothing for the boy. When Big Jim finally realized this, his indecision evaporated. He would sell out and try his fortunes in Arizona, where his sister Jane lived, the sister who had never seen Little Jim, but who had often written to Big Jim, inviting him to come and bring his family for a visit.

Big Jim had enough money from the sale of his effects to make the journey by train, even after he had deposited half of the proceeds at the local bank, in his wife's name. But being a true son of the open, he wanted to see the country; so he decided to travel horseback, with a pack-animal. Little Jim, used to the saddle, would find the journey a real adventure. They would take it easy. There was no reason for haste.

It had seemed the simplest thing to do, to sell out, leave that part of the country, and forget what had happened. There was nothing to be gained by staying where they were. Big Jim had lost his interest in the ranch. Moreover, there had been some talk of another man, in Laramie, a man who had "kept company" with Jenny Simpson, before she became Mrs. Jim Hastings. Mrs. Hastings was still young and quite good-looking.

It had seemed a simple thing to do—to leave and begin life over again in another land. But Big Jim had forgotten Smiler. Smiler was a dog of vague ancestry, a rough-coated, yellow dog that belonged solely to Little Jim. Smiler stuck so closely to Little Jim that their shadows were veritably one. Smiler was a sort of chuckle-headed, good-natured animal, meek, so long as Little Jim's prerogatives were not infringed upon, but a cyclone of yellow wrath if Little Jim were approached by any one in other than a friendly spirit. Even when Big Jim "roughed" his small son, in fun, Smiler grew nervous and bristled, and once, when the mother had smacked Little Jim for some offense or other, Smiler had taken sides to the extent of jumping between the mother and the boy, ready to do instant battle if his young partner were struck again.

"I'm afraid we can't take Smiler with us," said Big Jim, as Little Jim scurried about next morning, getting ready for the great adventure.

Little Jim stopped as though he had run against a rope. He had not even dreamed but that Smiler would go with them.

Now, Little Jim had not forgathered with punchers and townsfolk for nothing. He was naturally shrewd, and he did not offer or controvert opinions hastily. He stood holding a bit of old tie-rope in his hand, pondering this last unthinkable development of the situation. Smiler was to be left behind. Jimmy wanted to ask why Smiler could not go. He wanted to assure his father that Smiler would be a help rather than a hindrance to the expedition.

Little Jim knew that if he wept, his father might pay some attention to that sort of plea. But Little Jim did not intend to weep, nor ask questions, nor argue. Smiler stood expectantly watching the preparations. He knew that something important was about to happen, and, with the loyalty of his kind, he was ready to follow, no matter where. Smiler had sniffed the floor of the empty house, the empty stables, the corral. His folks were going somewhere. Well, he was ready.

Little Jim, who had been gazing wistfully at Smiler, suddenly strode to his pack and sat down. He bit his lips.

Henry Herbert Knibbs

Tears welled to his eyes and drifted slowly down his cheeks. He had not intended to let himself weep—but there was Smiler, wagging his thick tail, waiting to go.

"I g-g-guess you better go ahead and hit the trail, dad."

"Why, that's what we're going to do. What—" Big Jim glanced at his boy. "What's the matter?"

Little Jim did not answer, but his attitude spoke for itself. He had decided to stay with Smiler.

Big Jim frowned. It was the first time that the boy had ever openly rebelled. And because it was the first time, Big Jim realized its significance. Yet, such loyalty, even to a dog, was worth while.

Big Jim put his hand on Little Jim's shoulder. "Smiler'll get sore feet on the trails, Jimmy. And there won't be a whole lot to eat."

Little Jim blinked up at his father. "Well, he can have half of my grub, and I reckon I can pack him on the saddle with me if his feet get tender."

"All right. But don't blame me if Smiler peters out on the trip."

"Smiler's tough, he is!" stated Little Jim. "He's so tough he bites barb wire. Anyhow, you said we was goin' to take it easy. And he can catch rabbits, I guess."

"Perhaps he won't want to come along," suggested Big Jim as he pulled up a cincha and slipped the end through the ring.

Little Jim beckoned to Smiler who had stood solemnly

listening to the controversy about himself as though he understood. Smiler trotted over to Jimmy.

"You want to take it plumb easy on this trip," said Little Jim, "and not go to chasin' around and runnin' yourself ragged gettin' nowhere. If you get sore feet, we'll just have to beef you and hang your hide on the fence."

Smiler grinned and wagged his tail. He pushed up and suddenly licked Little Jim's face. Little Jim promptly cuffed him. Smiler came back for more.

Big Jim turned and watched the boy and the dog in their rough-and-tumble about the yard. He blinked and turned back to the horses. "Come on, Jimmy. We're all set."

"Got to throw my pack on ole Lazy, dad. Gimme a hand, will you?"

Little Jim never would admit that he could not do anything there was to be done. When he was stuck he simply asked his father to help him.

Big Jim slung up the small pack and drew down the hitch. Little Jim ducked under Lazy and took the rope on the other side, passing the end to his father.

"Reckon that pack'll ride all right," said the boy, surveying the outfit. "Got the *morrals* and everything, dad?"

"All set, Jimmy."

"Then let's go. I got my ole twenty-two loaded. If we run on to one of them stingin' lizards, he's sure a sconer. Does dogs eat lizards?"

Henry Herbert Knibbs

Big Jim swung to the saddle and hazed the old pack-horse ahead. "Don't know, Jimmy. Sometimes the Indians eat them."

"Eat stingin' lizards?"

"Yep."

"Well, I guess Smiler can, then. Come on, ole-timer!"

Suddenly Little Jim thought of his mother. It seemed that she ought to be with them. Little Jim had wept when Smiler was in question. Now he gazed with clear-eyed faith at his father.

"It ain't our fault ma ain't goin' with us, is it?" he queried timidly.

Big Jim shrugged his shoulders.

"Say, dad, we're headed west. Thought you said we was goin' to Arizona?"

"We'll turn south, after a while."

Little Jim asked no more questions. His father knew everything—why they were going and where. Little Jim glanced back to where Smiler padded along, his tongue out and his eyes already rimmed with dust, for he would insist upon traveling tight to Lazy's heels.

Little Jim leaned back. "Stick it out, ole-timer! But don't you go to cuttin' dad's trail till he gets kind of used to seein' you around. Sabe?"

Smiler grinned through a dust-begrimed countenance. He wagged his tail.

Little Jim plunked his horse in the ribs and drew up beside his father. Little Jim felt big and important riding beside his dad. There had been some kind of trouble at home—and they were leaving it behind. It would be a long trail, and his father sure would need help.

Little Jim drew a deep breath. He wanted to express his unwavering loyalty to his father. He wanted to talk of his willingness to go anywhere and share any kind of luck. But his resolve to speak evaporated in a sigh of satisfaction. This was a real holiday, an adventure. "Smiler's makin' it fine, dad."

But Big Jim did not seem to hear. He was gazing ahead, where in the distance loomed an approaching figure on horseback. Little Jim knew who it was, and was about to say so when his father checked him with a gesture. Little Jim saw his father shift his belt round so that his gun hung handy. He said nothing and showed by no other sign that he had recognized the approaching rider, who came on swiftly, his high-headed pinto fighting the bit.

Within twenty yards of them, the rider reined his horse to a walk. Little Jim saw the two men eye each other closely. The man on the pinto rode past. Little Jim turned to his father.

"I guess Panhandle is goin' to town," said the boy, not knowing just what to say, yet feeling that the occasion called for some remark.

"Panhandle" Sears and his father knew each other. They had passed on the road, neither speaking to the other. And Little Jim was not blind to the significant movement of shifting a belt that a gun might hang ready to hand.

Yet he soon forgot the incident in visioning the future.

Henry Herbert Knibbs

Arizona, Aunt Jane, and stingin' lizards!

Big Jim rode with head bowed. He was thinking of the man who had just passed them. If it had not been for the boy, Big Jim and that man would have had it out, there on the road. And Jenny Hastings would have been the cause of their quarrel. "Panhandle" Sears had "kept company" with Jenny before she became Big Jim's wife. Now that she had left him—

Big Jim turned and gazed back along the road. A far-away cloud of dust rolled toward the distant town of Laramie.

CHAPTER III

A MINUTE TOO LATE

The Overland, westbound, was late. Nevertheless, it had to stop at Antelope, but it did so grudgingly and left with a snort of disdain for the cow-town of the high mesa. Curious-eyed tourists had a brief glimpse of a loading-chute, cattle-pens, a puncher or two, and an Indian freighter's wagon just pulling in from the spaces, and accompanied by a plodding cavalcade of outriders on paint ponies.

Incidentally the westbound left one of those momentarily interested Easterners on the station platform, without baggage, sense of direction, or companion. He had stepped off the train to send a telegram to a friend in California. He discovered that he had left his address book in his grip. Meanwhile the train had moved forward some sixty yards, to take water. Returning for his address book, he boarded the wrong Pullman, realized his mistake, and hastened on through to his car. Out to the station again—delay in getting the attention of the telegraph operator, the wire finally written—and the Easterner heard the rumble of the train as it pulled out.

Even then he would have made it had it not been for a portly individual in shirt-sleeves who inadvertently blocked the

Henry Herbert Knibbs

doorway of the telegraph office. Bartley bumped into this portly person, tried to squeeze past, did so, and promptly caromed off the station agent whom he met head on, halfway across the platform. Gazing at the departing train, Bartley reached in his pocket for a cigar which he lighted casually.

The portly individual touched him on the shoulder. "'Nother one, this afternoon."

"Thanks. But my baggage is on that one."

"You're lucky it ain't two sections behind, this time of year. Travel is heavy."

Bartley's quick glance took in the big man from his high-heeled boots to his black Stetson. A cattleman, evidently well to do, and quite evidently not flustered by the mishaps of other folks.

"There's a right comfortable little hotel, just over there," stated the cattleman. "Wishful runs her. It ain't a bad place to wait for your train."

Bartley smiled in spite of his irritation.

The cattleman's eyes twinkled. "You'll be sending a wire to have 'em take care of your war bag. Well, come on in and send her. You can catch Number Eight about Winslow."

The cattleman forged ahead, and in the telegraph office, got the immediate attention of the operator, who took Bartley's message.

The cattleman paid for it. "'Tain't the first time my size has cost me money," he said, as Bartley protested. "Now, let's go over and get another cigar. Then we can mill around and see

Wishful. You'll like Wishful. He's different."

They strode down the street and stopped in at a saloon where the cattleman called for cigars. Bartley noticed that the proprietor of the place addressed the big cattleman as "Senator."

"This here is a dry climate, and a cigar burns up right quick, if you don't moisten it a little," said the cattleman. "I 'most always moisten mine."

Bartley grinned. "I think the occasion calls for it, Senator."

"Oh, shucks! Just call me Steve—Steve Brown. And just give us a little Green River Tom."

A few minutes later Bartley and his stout companion were seated on the veranda of the hotel, gazing out across the mesas. They were both comfortable, and quite content to watch the folk go past, out there in the heat. Bartley wondered if the title "Senator" were a nickname, or if the portly gentleman placidly smoking his cigar and gazing into space was really a politician.

A dusty cow-puncher drifted past the hotel, waving his hand to the Senator, who replied genially. A little later a Navajo buck rode up on a quick-stepping pony. He grunted a salutation and said something in his native tongue. The Senator replied in kind. Bartley was interested. Presently the Navajo dug his heels into his pony's ribs, and clattered up the road.

The Senator turned to Bartley. "Politics and cattle," he said, smiling.

Having learned the Senator's vocation, Bartley gave his own

as briefly. The Senator nodded.

"It is as obvious as all that, then?" queried Bartley.

"I wouldn't say that," stated the Senator carefully. "But after you bumped into me, and then stepped into the agent, and then turned around and took in my scenery, noticin' the set of my legs, I says to myself, 'painter-man or writer.' It was kind of in your eye. I figured you wa'n't no painter-man when you looked at the oil paintin' over the bar.

"A painter-man would 'a' looked sad or said somethin', for that there paintin' is the most gosh-awful picture of what a puncher might look like after a cyclone had hit him. I took a painter-man in there once, to get a drink. He took one look at that picture, and then he says, kind of sorrowful: 'Is this the only place in town where they serve liquor?' I told him it was. 'Let's go over and tackle the pump,' he says. But we had our drink. I told him just to turn his back on that picture when he took his."

"I might be anything but a writer," said Bartley.

"That's correct. But you ain't."

"You hit the nail on the head. However, I can't just follow your line of reasoning it out."

"Easy. Elimination. Now a tourist, regular, stares at folks and things. But a painter or writer he takes things in without starin'. There's some difference. I knew you were a man who did things. It's in your eye."

"Well," laughed Bartley, "I took you for a cattleman the minute I saw you."

"Which was a minute too late, eh?"

"I don't know about that. Since I've been sitting here looking at the mesa and those wonderful buttes over there, and watching the natives come and go, I have begun to feel that I don't care so much about that train, after all. I like this sort of thing. You see, I planned to visit California, but there was nothing definite about the plan. I chose California because I had heard so much about it. It doesn't matter much where I go. By the way, my name is Bartley."

"I'm Steve Brown—cattle and politics. I tell you, Mr. Bartley—"

"Suppose you say just Bartley?"

The Senator chuckled. "Suppose I said 'Green River'?"

"I haven't an objection in the world," laughed Bartley.

"Wishful, here, don't keep liquor," explained the Senator. "And he's right about that. Folks that stay at this hotel want to sleep nights."

The Senator heaved himself out of his chair, stood up, and stretched.

"I reckon you'll be wantin' to see all you can of this country. My ranch lays just fifty miles south of the railroad, and not a fence from here to there. Then, there's them Indians, up north a piece. And over yonder is where they dig up them prehistoric villages. And those buttes over there used to be volcanoes, before they laid off the job. To the west is the petrified forest. I made a motion once, when the Legislature was in session, to have that forest set aside as a buryin'-ground for politicians,—State Senators and the like,—but

Henry Herbert Knibbs

they voted me down. They said I didn't specify *dead* politicians.

"South of my place is the Apache reservation. There's good huntin' in that country. 'Course, Arizona ain't no Garden of Eden to some folks. Two kinds of folks don't love this State a little bit'—homesteaders and tourists. But when it comes to cattle and sheep and mines, you can't beat her. She sure is the Tiger Lily of the West. But let's step over and see Tom. Excuse me a minute. There's a constituent who has somethin' on his chest. I'll meet you at the station."

The Senator stepped out and talked with his constituent. Meanwhile, Bartley turned to gaze down the street. A string of empty freight wagons, followed by a lazy cloud of dust, rolled slowly toward town. Here and there a bit of red showed in the dun mass of riders that accompanied the wagons. A gay-colored blanket flickered in the sun. The mesas radiated keen dry heat.

Bartley turned and crossed over to the station. He blinked the effects of the white light from his eyes as he entered the telegraph office. The operator, in shirt-sleeves, and smoking a brown-paper cigarette, nodded and handed Bartley a service message stating that his effects would be carried to Los Angeles and held for further orders.

"It's sure hot," said the operator. "Did you want to send another wire?"

Bartley shook his head. "Who is that stout man I bumped into trying to catch my train?"

"That's Senator Steve Brown—State Senator. Thought you knew him."

"No. I just met him to-day."

The operator slumped down in his chair.

Bartley strode to the door and blinked in the Arizona sunshine. "By George!" he murmured, "I always thought they wore those big Stetsons for show. But all day in this sun—guess I'll have to have one."

CHAPTER IV

"A LITTLE GREEN RIVER"

To suddenly stop off at a cow-town station, without baggage or definite itinerary, was unconventional, to say the least. Bartley was amused and interested. Hitherto he had written more or less conventional stuff—acceptable stories of the subway, the slums, the docks, and the streets of Eastern cities. But now, as he strode over to the saloon, he forgot that he was a writer of stories. A boyish longing possessed him to see much of the life roundabout, even to the farthest, faint range of hills—and beyond.

He felt that while he still owed something to his original plan of visiting California, he could do worse than stay right where he was. He had thought of wiring to have his baggage sent back. Then it occurred to him that, aside from his shaving-kit and a few essentials, his baggage comprised but little that he could use out here in the mesa country. And he felt a certain relief in not having trunks to look after. Outing flannels and evening clothes would hardly fit into the present scheme of things. The local store would furnish him all that he needed. In this frame of mind he entered the Blue Front Saloon where he found Senator Steve and his foreman seated at a side table discussing the merits of "Green River."

"Hello!" called the Senator. "Mr. Bartley, meet my foreman, Lon Pelly."

They shook hands.

"Lon says the source of Green River is Joy in the Hills," asserted the Senator, smiling.

The long, lean cow-puncher grinned. "Steve, here, says the source of Green River is trouble."

"Now, as a writin' man, what would you say?" queried the Senator.

Bartley gazed at the label on the bottle under discussion. "Well, as a writer, I might say that it depends how far you travel up or down Green River. But as a mere individual enjoying the blessings of companionship, I should say, let's experiment, judiciously."

"Fetch a couple more glasses, Tom," called the Senator.

After the essential formalities, Bartley pushed back his chair, crossed one leg over the other, and lighted a cigar. "I'm rather inclined toward that Joy in the Hills theory, just now," he asserted.

"That's all right," said Lon Pelly. "Bein' a little inclined don't hurt any. But if you keep on reachin' for Joy, your foot is like to slip. Then comes Trouble."

"Lon's qualified for the finals once or twice," said the Senator. "Now, take *me*, for a horrible example. I been navigatin' Green River, off and on, for quite a spell, and I never got hung up bad."

"Speaking of rivers, they're rather scarce in this country, I believe," said Bartley.

"Yes. But some of 'em are noticeable in the rainy season," stated Senator Steve. "But you ain't seen Arizona. You've only been peekin' through your fingers at her. Wait till you get on a cayuse and hit the trail for a few hundred miles— that's the only way to see the country. Now, take 'Cheyenne.' He rides this here country from Utah to the border, and he can tell you somethin' about Arizona.

"Cheyenne is a kind of hobo puncher that rides the country with his little old pack-horse, stoppin' by to work for a grubstake when he has to, but ramblin' most of the time. He used to be a top-hand once. Worked for me a spell. But he can't stay in one place long. Wish you could meet him sometime. He can tell you more about this State than any man I know. He's what you might call a character for a story. He stops by regular, at the ranch, mebby for a day or two, and then takes the trail, singin' his little old song. He's kind of a outdoor poet. Makes up his own songs."

"What was that one about Arizona that you gave 'em over to the State House onct?" queried Lon Pelly.

"Oh, that wa'n't Cheyenne's own po'try. It was one he read in a magazine that he gave me. Let's see—

"Arizona! The tramp of cattle,
The biting dust and the raw, red brand:
Shuffling sheep and the smoke of battle:
The upturned face—and the empty hand.

"Dawn and dusk, and the wide world singing,
Songs that thrilled with the pulse of life,
As we clattered down with our rein chains ringing

To woo you—but never to make you wife."

The Senator smiled a trifle apologetically. "There's more of it. But po'try ain't just in my line. Once in a while I bust loose on po'try—that is, my kind of po'try. And I want to say that we sure clattered down from the Butte and the Blue in the old days, with our rein chains jinglin', thinkin'—some of us—that Arizona was ours to fare-ye-well.

"But we old-timers lived to find out that Arizona was too young to get married yet; so we just had to set back and kind of admire her, after havin' courted her an amazin' lot, in our young days." The Senator chuckled. "Now, Lon, here, he'll tell you that there ain't no po'try in this here country. And I never knew they was till I got time to set back and think over what we unbranded yearlin's used to do."

"For instance?" queried Bartley.

Senator Steve waved his pudgy hand as though shooing a flock of chickens off a front lawn. "If I was to tell you some of the things that happened, you would think I was a heap sight bigger liar than I am. Seein' some of them yarns in print, folks around this country would say: 'Steve Brown's corralled some tenderfoot and loaded him to the muzzle with shin tangle and ancient history!' Things that would seem amazin' to you would never ruffle the hair of the mavericks that helped make this country."

"This country ain't all settled yet," said the foreman, rising. "Reckon I'll step along, Steve."

After the foreman had departed, Bartley turned to the Senator. "Are there many more like him, out here?"

"Who, Lon? Well, a few. He's been foreman for me quite a

spell. Lon he thinks. And that's more than I ever did till after I was thirty. And Lon ain't twenty-six, yet."

"I think I'll step over to the drug-store and get a few things," said Bartley.

"So you figure to bed down at the hotel, eh?"

"Yes. For a few days, at least. I want to get over the idea that I have to take the next train West before I make any further plans."

The Senator accompanied Bartley to the drug-store. The Easterner bought what he needed in the way of shaving-kit and brush and comb. The Senator excused himself and crossed the street to talk to a friend. The afternoon sun slanted across the hot roofs, painting black shadows on the dusty street. Bartley found Wishful, the proprietor, and told him that he would like to engage a room with a bath.

Wishful smiled never a smile as he escorted Bartley to a room.

"I'll fetch your bath up, right soon," he said solemnly.

Presently Wishful appeared with a galvanized iron washtub and a kettle of boiling water. Bartley thanked him.

"You can leave 'em out in the hall when you're through," said Wishful.

Bartley enjoyed a refreshing bath and rub-down. Later he set the kettle and tub out in the dim hallway. Then he sat down and wrote a letter to his friend in California, explaining his change of plan. The afternoon sunlight waned. Bartley gazed out across the vast mesas, lavender-hued and wonderful, as they darkened to blue, then to purple that was shot with strange half-lights from the descending sun.

Suddenly a giant hand seemed to drop a canopy over the vista, and it was night. Bartley lighted the oil lamp and sat staring out into the darkness. From below came the rattle of dishes. Presently Bartley heard heavy, deliberate footsteps ascending the stairway. Then a clanging crash and a thud, right outside his door. He flung the door open. Senator Steve was rising from the flattened semblance of a washtub and feeling of himself tenderly. The Senator blinked, surveyed the wrecked tub and the kettle silently, and then without comment he stepped back and kicked the kettle. It soared and dropped clanging into the hall below.

Wishful appeared at the foot of the stairs. "Did you ring, Senator?"

"Yes, I did! And I'm goin' to ring again."

"Hold on!" said Wishful, "I'll come up and get the tub. I got the kettle."

The Senator puffed into Bartley's room and sat on the edge of the bed. He wiped his bald head, smiling cherubically. "Did you hear him, askin' me, a member of the Society for the Prevention of Progress, if I rang for him! That's about all the respect I command in this community. I sure want to apologize for not stoppin' to knock," added the Senator.

Bartley grinned. "It was hardly necessary. I heard you."

"I just came up to see if you would take dinner with me and my missus. We're goin' to eat right soon. You see, my missus never met up with a real, live author."

"Thanks, Senator. I'll be glad to meet your family. But suppose you forget that author stuff and just take me as a tenderfoot out to see the sights. I'll like it better."

"Why, sure! And while the House is in session, I might rise to remark that I can't help bein' called 'Senator,' because I'm guilty. But, honest, I always feel kinder toward my fellow-bein's who call me just plain 'Steve.'"

"All right. I'll take your word for it."

"Don't you take my word for anything. How do you know but I might be tryin' to sell you a gold mine?"

"I think the risk would be about even," said Bartley.

The Senator chuckled. "I just heard Wishful lopin' down the hall with his bathin' outfit, so I guess the right of way is clear again. And there goes the triangle—sounds like the old ranch, that triangle. You see, Wishful used to be a cow-hand, and lots of cow-hands stop at this hotel when they're in town. That triangle sounds like home to 'em. I'm stoppin' here myself. But I got a real bathroom out to the ranch. Let's go down and look at some beef on the plate."

CHAPTER V

"TOP HAND ONCE"

Bartley happened to be alone on the veranda of the Antelope House that evening. Senator Brown and his "missus" had departed for their ranch. Mrs. Senator Brown had been a bit diffident when first meeting Bartley, but he soon put her at her ease with some amusing stories of Eastern experiences. The dinner concluded with an invitation from Mrs. Brown that anticipated Bartley visiting the ranch and staying as long as he wished. The day following the Senator's departure Bartley received a telegram from his friend in California, wishing him good luck and a pleasant journey in the Arizona country. The friend would see to Bartley's baggage, as Bartley had forwarded the claim checks in his letter.

The town was quiet and the stars were serenely brilliant. The dusty, rutted road past the hotel, dim gray in the starlight, muffled the tread of an occasional Navajo pony passing in the faint glow of light from the doorway. Bartley was content with things as he found them, just then. But he knew that he would eventually go away from there—from the untidy town, the railroad, the string of box-cars on the siding, and seek the new, the unexpected, an experience to be had only by kicking loose from convention and stepping out for himself. He thought of writing a Western story. He realized that all he knew of the West was from hearsay, and a brief contact with actual Westerners. He would do better to go out in the fenceless land and live a story, and then write it. And better still, he would let chance decide where and when he would go.

His first intimation that chance was in his vicinity was the distant, faint cadence of a song that floated over the night-black mesa from the north. Presently he heard the soft, muffled tread of horses and a distinct word or two of the song. He leaned forward, interested, amused, alert. The voice was a big voice, mellowed by distance. There was a take-it-or-leave-it swing to the melody that suggested the singer's absolute oblivion to anything but the joy of singing. Again the plod, plod of the horses, and then:

> I was top-hand once for the T-Bar-T,
> In the days of long ago,
> But I took to seein' the scenery
> Where the barbed-wire fence don't grow.

> I was top-hand once—but the trail for mine,
> And plenty of room to roam;
> So now I'm ridin' the old chuck line,
> And any old place is home ... for me ...
> And any old place is home.

Bartley grinned. Whoever he was, drifting in from the northern spaces, he had evidently lost the pack-horse that bore his troubles. Suddenly, out of the wall of dusk that edged the strip of road loomed a horse's head, and then another. The lead horse bore a pack. The second horse was ridden by an individual who leaned slightly forward, his hands clasped comfortably over the saddle horn. The horses stopped in the light of the doorway.

"Well, I reckon we're here," said a voice. "But hotels and us ain't in the same class. I stop at the Antelope House, take a look at her, and then spread my roll in the brush, same as always. Nobody to home? They don't know what they're missin'."

Bartley struck a match and lighted his cigar. The pack-horse jerked its head up.

"Hello, stranger! Now I didn't see you settin' there."

"Good-evening! But why 'stranger' when you say you can't see me?"

"Why? 'Cause everybody knows *me*, and you didn't whoop when I rode up. Me, I'm Cheyenne, from no place, and likewise that's where I'm goin'. This here town of Antelope got in the way—towns is always gittin' in my way—but nobody can help that. Is Wishful bedded down for the night or is he over to the Blue Front shootin' craps?"

"I couldn't say. I seem to be the only one around here, just now."

"That sure excuses me and the hosses. Wishful is down to the Blue Front, all right. It's the only exercise he gets, regular." Cheyenne pushed back the brim of his faded black Stetson and sighed heavily. Bartley caught a glimpse of a face as care-free as that of a happy child—the twinkle of humorous eyes and a flash of white teeth as the other grinned. "Reckon you never heard tell of me," said the rider, hooking his leg over the horn.

I just arrived yesterday. I have not heard of you—but I heard you down the road, singing. I like that song."

"One of my own. Yes, I come into town singin' and I go out singin'. 'Course, we eat, when it's handy. Singin' sure keeps a fellow's appetite from goin' to sleep. Guess I'll turn the hosses into Wishful's corral and go find him. Reckon you had your dinner."

"Several hours ago."

"Well, I had mine this mornin'. The dinner I had this mornin' was the one I ought to had day before yesterday. But I aim to catch up—and mebby get ahead a couple of eats, some day. But the hosses get theirs, regular. Come on, Filaree, we'll go prospect the sleepin'-quarters."

Bartley sat back and smiled to himself as Cheyenne departed for the corral. This wayfarer, breezing in from the spaces, suggested possibilities as a character for a story No doubt the song was more or less autobiographical. "A top-hand once, but the trail for mine," seemed to explain the singer's somewhat erratic dinner schedule. Bartley thought that he would like to see more of this strange itinerant, who sang both coming into and going out of town.

Presently Cheyenne was back, singing something about a Joshua tree as he came.

He stopped at the veranda rail. His smile was affable. "Guess I'll go over and hunt up Wishful. I reckon you'll have to excuse me for not refusin' to accompany you to the Blue Front to get a drink."

Bartley was puzzled. "Would you mind saying that again?"

"Sure I don't mind. I thought, mebby, you bein' a stranger, settin' there alone and lookin' at the dark, that you was kind of lonesome. I said I reckoned you'd have to excuse me for not refusin' to go over to the Blue Front and take a drink."

"I think I get you. I'll buy. I'll try anything, once."

Cheyenne grinned. "I kind of hate to drink alone, 'specially when I'm broke."

Bartley grinned in turn. "So do I. I suppose it is all right to leave. The door is wide open and there doesn't seem to be any one in charge.

"She sure is an orphan, to-night. But, honest, Mr.—"

"Bartley."

"Mr. Bartley, nobody'd ever think of stealin' anything from Wishful. Everybody likes Wishful 'round here. And strangers wouldn't last long that tried to lift anything from his tepee. That is, not any longer than it would take Wishful to pull a gun—and that ain't long."

"If he caught them."

"Caught 'em? Say, stranger, how far do you think a man could travel out of here, before somebody'd get him? Anyhow, Wishful ain't got nothin' in his place worth stealin'."

"Wishful doesn't look very warlike," said Bartley.

"Nope. That's right. He looks kind of like he'd been hit on the roof and hadn't come to, yet. But did you ever see him shoot craps?"

"No."

"Then you've got somethin' comin', besides buyin' me a drink."

Bartley laughed as he stepped down to the road. Bartley, a fair-sized man, was surprised to realize that the other was all of a head taller than himself. Cheyenne had not looked it in the saddle.

"Are you acquainted with Senator Brown?" queried Bartley as he strode along beside the stiff-gaited outlander.

Cheyenne stopped and pushed back his hat. "Senator Steve Brown? Say, pardner, me and Steve put this here country on the map. If kings was in style, Steve would be wearin' a crown. Why, last election I wore out a pair of jeans lopin' around this here country campaignin' for Steve. See this hat? Steve give me this hat—a genuwine J.B., the best they make. Inside he had printed on the band, in gold, 'From Steve to Cheyenne, hoping it will always fit.' Do I know Steve Brown? Next time you see him just ask him about Cheyenne Hastings."

"I met the Senator, yesterday. Come to think of it, he did mention your name—'Cheyenne—and said you knew the country."

"Was you lookin' for a guide, mebby?"

"Well, not exactly. But I hope to see something of Arizona."

"Uh-huh. Well, I travel alone, mostly. But right now I'm flat broke. If you was headin' south—"

"I expect to visit Mr. and Mrs. Brown some day. Their ranch is south of here, I believe."

"Yep. Plumb south, on the Concho road. I'm ridin' down that way."

"Well, we will talk about it later," said Bartley as they entered the saloon.

With a few exceptions, the men in the place were grouped round a long table, in the far end of the room, at the head of which stood Wishful evidently about to make a throw with the dice. No one paid the slightest attention to the arrival of Bartley and his companion, with the exception of the proprietor, who nodded to Bartley and spoke a word of greeting to Cheyenne.

Bartley did the honors which included a sandwich and a glass of beer for Cheyenne, who leaned with his elbow on the bar gazing at the men around the table. Out of the corner of his eye Bartley saw the proprietor touch Cheyenne's arm and, leaning across the bar, whisper something to him. Cheyenne straightened up and seemed to be adjusting his belt. Bartley caught a name: "Panhandle." He turned and glanced at Cheyenne.

The humorous expression had faded from Cheyenne's face and in its stead there was a sort of grim, speculative line to the mouth, and no twinkle in the blue eyes. Bartley stepped over to the long table and watched the game. Craps, played by these free-handed sons of the open, had more of a punch than he had imagined possible. A pile of silver and bills lay on the table—a tidy sum—no less than two hundred dollars.

Wishful, the sad-faced, seemed to be importuning some one by the name of "Jimmy Hicks" to make himself known, as the dice rattled across the board. The players laughed as Wishful relinquished the dice. A lean outlander, with a scarred face, took up the dice and made a throw. He evidently did not want to locate an individual called "Little Joe," whom he importuned incessantly to stay away.

Side bets were made and bills and silver withdrawn or added to the pile with a rapidity which amazed Bartley. Hitherto craps had meant to him three or four newsboys in an alley and a little pile of nickels and pennies. But this game was of robust proportions. It had pep and speed.

Bartley became interested. His fingers itched to grasp the dice and try his luck. But he realized that his amateurish knowledge of the game would be an affront to those free-moving sons of the mesa. So he contented himself with watching the game and the faces of the men as they won or lost. Bartley felt that some one was close behind him looking over his shoulder. Cheyenne's eyes were fixed on the player known as "Panhandle," and on no other person at that table. Bartley turned back to the game.

Just then some one recognized Cheyenne and spoke his name. The game stopped and Bartley saw several of the men glance curiously from Cheyenne to the man known as "Panhandle." Then the game was resumed, but it was a quieter game. One or two of the players withdrew.

"Play a five for me," said Bartley, turning to Cheyenne.

"I'll do that—fifty-fifty," said Cheyenne as Bartley stepped back and handed him a bill.

Cheyenne straightway elbowed deeper into the group and finally secured the dice. Wishful, for some unknown reason, remarked that he would back Cheyenne to win—"shootin' with either hand," Wishful concluded. Bartley noticed that again one or two players withdrew and strolled to the bar. Meanwhile, Cheyenne threw and sang a little song to himself.

His throws were wild, careless, and lucky. Slowly he accumulated easy wealth. His forehead was beaded with sweat. His eyes glistened. He forgot his song. Bartley stepped over to the bar and chatted for a few minutes with the proprietor, mentioning Senator Steve and his wife.

When Bartley returned to the game the players had dwindled to a small group—'Wishful, the man called "Panhandle," a fat Mexican, a railroad engineer, and Cheyenne.

Bartley turned to a bystander.

"Cheyenne seems to be having all the luck," he said.

"Is he a friend of yours?"

"Never saw him until to-night."

"He ain't as lucky as you think," stated the other significantly.

"How is that?"

"Panhandle, the man with the scar on his face, ain't no friend of Cheyenne's."

"Oh, I see."

Bartley turned from the man, and watched the players. Wishful had withdrawn from the game, but he stood near the table, watching closely. Presently the fat Mexican quit playing and left. Cheyenne threw and won. He played as though the dice were his and he was giving an exhibition for the benefit of the other players. Finally the engineer quit, and counted his winnings. Cheyenne and the man, Panhandle, faced each other, with Bartley standing close to Cheyenne and Wishful, who had moved around the table, standing close to Panhandle.

Panhandle took up the dice. There was no joy in his play. He shot the dice across the table viciously. Every throw was a, sort of insidious insult to his competitor, Cheyenne. Bartley was more interested in the performance than the actual winning or losing, although he realized that Cheyenne was still a heavy winner.

Presently Wishful stepped over to Bartley and touched his arm. Panhandle and Cheyenne were intent upon their game.

"You kin see better from that side of the table," said Wishful mildly, yet with a peculiar significance.

Bartley glanced up, his face expressing bewilderment.

"I seen you slip Cheyenne a bill," murmured Wishful. "Accordin' to that, you're backin' him. Thought I'd just mention it."

"I don't understand what you're driving at," said Bartley.

"That's just why I spoke to you." And Wishful's face expressed a sort of sad wonder. But then, the Easterner had not been in town long and he did not know Panhandle.

Wishful turned away casually. Bartley noticed that he again took up his position near Panhandle.

This time Panhandle glanced up and asked Wishful if he didn't want to come into the game.

Wishful shook his head. "No use tryin' to bust his luck," he said, indicating Cheyenne.

"Oh, I don't know," said Panhandle.

"And he's got good backin'," continued Wishful.

Panhandle slanted a narrow glance toward Bartley, and Bartley felt that the other had somehow or other managed to convey an insult and a challenge in that glance, which suggested the contempt of the tough Westerner for the supposedly tender Easterner.

Bartley did not know just what was on the boards, aside from dice and money, but he took Wishful's hint and moved around to Panhandle's side of the table, leaving Cheyenne facing his competitor alone. Bartley happened to catch Cheyenne's eye. The happy-go-lucky expression was gone. Cheyenne's face seemed troubled, yet he played with his former vigor and luck.

Panhandle posed insolently, his thumb in his belt, watching the dice. He was all but broke. Cheyenne kept rolling the bones, but now he evoked no aid from the gods of African golf. His lips were set in a thin line.

Suddenly he tossed up the dice, caught them and transferred them to his right hand. Hitherto he had been shooting with his left. "I'll shoot you, either hand," he said.

"And win," murmured Wishful.

Panhandle whirled and confronted Wishful. "I don't see any of your money on the table," he snarled.

"I'll come in—on the next game," stated Wishful mildly.

Panhandle's last dollar was on the table. He reached forward and drew a handful of bills from the pile and counted them.

"Fifty," he said; "fifty against the pot that you don't make your next throw."

"Suits me," said Cheyenne, picking up the dice and shaking them.

Cheyenne threw and won on the third try. Panhandle reached toward the pile of money again.

Cheyenne, who had not picked up the dice, stopped him. "You can't play on that money," he stated tensely. "Half of it belongs to Mr. Bartley, there."

"What have you got to say about it," challenged Panhandle, turning to Bartley.

"Half of the money on the table is mine, according to agreement. I backed Cheyenne to win."

"No dam' tenderfoot can tell me where to head in!" exclaimed Panhandle. "Go on and shoot, you yella-bellied waddie!" And Panhandle reached toward the money.

"Just a minute," said Bartley quietly. "The game is finished."

"Take your mouth out of this, you dam' dude!"

"Put your gun on the table—and then tell me that," said Bartley.

Panhandle lowered his hand to his gun, hesitated, and then whirling, slapped Bartley's face.

Wishful, the silent, jerked out his own gun and rapped Panhandle on the head. Panhandle dropped in a heap.

It had happened so quickly that Bartley hardly realized what had happened. Panhandle was on the floor, literally down and out. Bartley was surprised that such an apparently light tap on the head should put a man out.

"Get him out of here," said Tom, the proprietor. "I don't want any rough stuff in here. And if I were in your boots, Cheyenne, I'd leave town for a while."

"I'm leavin' to-morrow mornin'." Cheyenne was coolly counting his winnings.

Wishful, the silent, doused a glass of water in Panhandle's face. Presently Panhandle was revived and helped from the saloon. His former attitude of belligerency had entirely evaporated. Wishful followed him to the hitch-rail and saw him mount his horse.

"Your best bet is to fan it back where you come from, and stay there," said Wishful softly. "You don't belong in this town, and you can't go slappin' any of my guests in the face and get away with it. And when you git so you can think it over, just figure that if I hadn't 'a' slowed you down, Cheyenne would 'a' killed you."

Panhandle did not feel like discussing the question just then. He left without even turning to glance back. If he had glanced back, he would have seen that Wishful had disappeared. Wishful, familiar with the ways of Panhandle and his kind, immediately sought the shadows, leaving the lighted doorway a blank. He entered the saloon from the rear.

Cheyenne was endeavoring to make Bartley take half of the winnings. "You staked me—and it's fifty-fifty, pardner," insisted Cheyenne.

Finally Bartley accepted his share of the money and stuffed it into his pocket.

"Now I can get back at you," stated Cheyenne, gesturing toward the bar.

His gesture included both Wishful and Bartley. Bartley, a bit shaken, accepted the invitation. Wishful, not at all shaken, but rather a bit more silent and melancholy than heretofore, also accepted.

Alone in his room at the hotel, Bartley wondered what would have happened if Wishful had not rapped Panhandle on the head. Bartley recalled the fact that he had drawn back his arm, intending to take one good punch at Panhandle, even if it were his last. But Panhandle had crumpled down suddenly, silently, and Wishful had stood over him, gazing down speculatively and swinging his gun back and forth before he returned it to the holster. "They move quick, in this country," thought Bartley. "And speaking of material for a story—" Then he smiled.

Somewhere out on the mesa Cheyenne had spread his bed-roll and was no doubt sleeping peacefully. Bartley shook his head. He had been in Antelope but two days and yet it seemed that months had passed since he had stepped from the westbound train to telegraph to his friend in California. Incidentally, he decided to purchase an automatic pistol.

CHAPTER VI

A HORSE-TRADE

When Bartley came down to breakfast next morning he noticed two horses tied at the hitch-rail in front of the hotel. One of the horses, a rather stocky gray, bore a pack. The other, a short-coupled, sturdy buckskin, was saddled. Evidently Cheyenne was trying to catch up with his dinner schedule, for as Bartley entered the dining-room he saw him, sitting face to face with a high stack of flapjacks, at the base of which reposed two fried eggs among some curled slivers of bacon.

Two railroad men, a red-eyed Eastern tourist who looked as though he had not slept for a week, a saturnine cattleman in from the mesas, and two visiting ladies from an adjacent town comprised the tale of guests that morning. As Bartley came in the guests glanced at him curiously. They had heard of the misunderstanding at the Blue Front.

Cheyenne immediately rose and offered Bartley a chair at his table. The two women, alone at their table, immediately became subdued and watchful. They were gazing their first upon an author. Wishful had made the fact known, with some pride. The ladies, whom Cheyenne designated as "cow-bunnies,"—or wives of ranchers,—were dressed in their "best clothes," and were trying to live up to them. They had about finished breakfast, and shortly after Bartley was seated they rose. On their way out they stopped at Cheyenne's table.

"Don't forget to stop by when you ride our way," said one of the women.

Bartley noticed the toil-worn hands, and the lines that hard work and worry had graven in her face. Her "best clothes" rather accentuated these details. But back of it all he sensed the resolute spirit of the West, resourceful, progressive, large-visioned.

"Meet Mr. Bartley," said Cheyenne unexpectedly.

Which was just what the two women had been itching to do. Bartley rose and shook hands with them.

"A couple of lady friends of mine," said Cheyenne when they had gone.

Cheyenne made no mention of the previous evening's game, or its climax. Yet Bartley had gathered from Wishful that Panhandle Sears and Cheyenne had an unsettled quarrel between them.

In the hotel office Cheyenne purchased cigars and proffered Bartley a half-dozen. Bartley took one. Cheyenne seemed disappointed. When cigars were going round, it seemed strange not to take full advantage of the circumstance. As they stepped out to the veranda, the horses recognized Cheyenne and nickered gently.

"Going south?" queried Bartley.

"That's me. I got the silver changed to bills and some of the bills changed to grub. I reckon I'll head south. Kind of wish you was headed that way."

Bartley bit the end from his cigar and lighted it, as he gazed out across the morning mesa. A Navajo buck loped past and jerked his little paint horse to a stop at the drug-store.

Cheyenne, pulling up a cinch, smiled at Bartley.

"That Injun was in a hurry till he got here. And he'll be in a hurry, leavin'. But you notice how easy he takes it right now. Injuns has got that dignity idea down fine."

"Did he come in for medicine, perhaps?"

"Mebby. But most like he's after chewin'-gum for his squaw, and cigarettes for himself, with a bottle of red pop on the side. Injuns always buy red pop."

"Cigarettes and chewing-gum?"

"Sure thing! Didn't you ever see a squaw chew gum and smoke a tailor-made cigarette at the same time? You didn't, eh? Well, then, you got somethin' comin'."

"Romance!" laughed Bartley.

"Ever sleep in a Injun hogan?" queried Cheyenne as he busied himself adjusting the pack.

"No. This is my first trip West."

"I was forgettin'. Well, I ain't what you'd call a dude, but, honest, if I was prospectin' round lookin' for Injun romance I'd use a pair of field-glasses. Injuns is all right if you're far enough up wind from 'em."

"When do you start?" asked Bartley.

"Oh, 'most any time. And that's when I'll get there."

"Well, give my regards to Senator Brown and his wife, if you happen to see them."

"Sure thing! I'm on my way. You know—

"I was top-hand once—but the trail for mine:
Git along, cayuse, git along!
But now I'm ridin' the old chuck line,
Feedin' good and a-feelin' fine:
Oh, some folks eat and some folks dine,
Git along, cayuse, git along!"

Bartley smiled. Here was the real hobo, the irrepressible absolute. Cheyenne stepped up and swung to the saddle with the effortless ease of the old hand. Bartley noticed that the pack-horse had no lead-rope, nor had he been tied. Bartley did not know that Filaree, the pack-horse, would never let Joshua, the saddle-horse, out of his sight. They had traveled the Arizona trails together for years.

In spite of his happy-go-lucky indifference to persons and events, Cheyenne had a sort of intuitive shrewdness in reading humans. And he read in Bartley's glance a half-awakened desire to outfit and hit the trail himself. But Cheyenne departed without suggesting any such idea. Every man for himself was his motto. "And as for me," he added, aloud:

Seems like I don't git anywhere,
Git along, cayuse, git along;
But we're leavin' here and we're goin' there:
Git along, cayuse, git along!

With little ole Josh that steps right free,
And my ole gray pack-hoss, Filaree,
The world ain't got no rope on me:
Git along, cayuse, git along!

Bartley watched him as he crossed the railroad tracks and turned down a side street.

Back in his room Bartley paced up and down, keeping time to the tune of Cheyenne's trail song. The morning sun poured down upon the station roof opposite, and danced flickering across the polished tracks of the railroad. Presently Bartley stopped pacing his room and stood at the window. Far out across the mesa he saw a rider, drifting along in the sunshine, followed by a gray pack-horse.

"By George!" exclaimed Bartley. "He may be a sort of wandering joke to the citizens of this State, but he's doing what he wants to do, and that's more than I'm doing. Just fifty miles to Senator Brown's ranch. Drop in and see us. As the chap in Denver said when he wrote to his friend in El Paso: 'Drop into Denver some evening and I'll show you the sights.' Distance? Negligible. Time? An inconsequent factor. Big stuff! As for me, I think I'll go downstairs and interview the pensive Wishful."

Wishful had the Navajo blankets and chairs piled up in the middle of the hotel office and was thoughtfully sweeping out cigar ashes, cigarette stubs, and burned matches. Wishful, besides being proprietor of the Antelope House, was chambermaid, baggage-wrangler, clerk, advertising manager, and, upon occasion, waiter in his own establishment. And he kept a neat place.

Bartley walked over to the desk. Wishful kept on sweeping. Bartley glanced at the signatures on the register. Near the bottom of the page he found Cheyenne's name, and opposite it "Arizona."

"Where does Cheyenne belong, anyway?" queried Bartley.

Wishful stopped sweeping and leaned on his broom. "Wherever he happens to be." And Wishful sighed and began sweeping again.

"What sort of traveling companion would he make?"

Wishful stopped sweeping. His melancholy gaze was fixed on a defunct cigar. "Never heard either of his hosses object to his company," he replied.

Bartley grinned and glanced up and down the register. Wishful dug into a corner with his broom. Something shot rattling across the floor. Wishful laid down the broom and upon hands and knees began a search. Presently he rose. A slow smile illumined his face. He had found a pair of dice in the litter on the floor. He made a throw, shook his head, and picked up the dice. His sweeping became more sprightly. Amused by the preoccupation of the lank and cautiously humorous Wishful, Bartley touched the bell on the desk. Wishful promptly stood his broom against the wall, rolled down his sleeves, and stepped behind the counter.

"I think I'll pay my bill," said Bartley.

Wishful promptly named the amount. Bartley proffered a ten-dollar bill.

Wishful searched in the till for change. He shook his head. "You got two dollars comin'," he stated.

"I'll shake you for that two dollars," said Bartley.

Wishful's tired eyes lighted up. "You said somethin'." And he produced the dice.

Just then the distant "Zoom" of the westbound Overland shook the silence. Wishful hesitated, then gestured magnificently toward space. What was the arrival of a mere train, with possibly a guest or so for the hotel, compared with a game of craps?

While they played, the train steamed in and was gone. Wishful won the two dollars.

Bartley escaped to the veranda and his reflections. Presently he rose and strolled round to the corral. Wishful's three saddle-animals were lazying in the heat. Bartley was not unfamiliar with the good points of a horse. He rejected the sorrel with the Roman nose, as stubborn and foolish. The flea-bitten gray was all horse, but he had a white-rimmed eye. The chestnut bay was a big, hardy animal, but he appeared rather slow and deliberate. Yet he had good, solid feet, plenty of bone, deep withers, and powerful hindquarters.

Bartley stepped round to the hotel. "Have you a minute to spare?" he queried as Wishful finished rearranging the furniture of the lobby.

Wishful had. He followed Bartley round to the corral.

"I'm thinking of buying a saddle-horse," stated Bartley.

Wishful leaned his elbows on the corral bar. "Why don't you rent one—and turn him in when you're through with him."

"I'd rather own one, and I may use him a long time."

"I ain't sufferin' to sell any of my hosses, Mr. Bartley. But I wouldn't turn down a fair offer."

"Set a price on that sorrel," said Bartley.

Now, Wishful was willing to part with the sorrel, which was showy and looked fast. Bartley did not want the animal. He merely wanted to arrive at a basis from which to work.

"Well," drawled Wishful, "I'd let him go for a hundred."

"What will you take for the gray?"

"Him? Well, he's the best hoss I got. I don't think he's your kind of a hoss."

"The best, eh? And a hundred for the sorrel." Bartley appeared to reflect.

Wishful really wanted to sell the gray, describing him as the best horse he owned to awaken Bartley's interest. The best horse in the corral was the big bay cow-horse; but Wishful had no idea that Bartley knew that.

"Would you put a price on the gray?" queried Bartley.

"Why, sure! You can have him, for a hundred and twenty-five."

"A hundred for the sorrel—and a hundred and twenty-five for the gray; is that correct?"

"Yep."

"And you say the gray is the best horse in the corral?"

"He sure is!"

"All right. I'll give you a hundred for that big bay, there. I don't want to rob you of your best horse, Wishful."

Wishful saw that he was cornered. He had cornered himself, premising that the Easterner didn't know horses. "That bay ain't much account, Mr. Bartley. He's slow—nothin' but a ole cow-hoss I kind of keep around for odd jobs of ropin' and such."

"Well, he's good enough for me. I'll give you a hundred for him."

Wishful scratched his head. He did not want to sell the bay for that sum, yet he was too good a sport to go back on his word.

"Say, where was you raised?" he queried abruptly.

"In Kentucky."

"Hell, I thought you was from New York?"

"I lived in Kentucky until I was twenty-five."

"Was your folks hoss-traders?"

"Not exactly," laughed Bartley. "My father always kept a few good saddle-horses, however."

"Uh-huh? I reckon he did. And you ain't forgot what a real hoss looks like, either." Wishful's pensive countenance lighted suddenly. "You'll be wantin' a rig—saddle and bridle and slicker and saddle-bags. Now I got just what you want."

Bartley stepped to the stable and inspected the outfit. It was old and worn, and worth, Bartley estimated, about thirty dollars, all told.

"I'll let you have the whole outfit—hoss and rig and all, for two hundred," stated Wishful unblushingly.

"I priced a saddle, over in the shop across from the station, this morning," said Bartley.

"With bridle and blanket and saddle-pockets it would only stand me ninety dollars. If the bay is the poorest horse you own, then at your figure this outfit would come rather high."

"I might 'a' knowed it!" stated Wishful. "Say, Mr. Bartley, give me a hundred and fifty for the hoss and I'll throw in the rig."

"No. I know friendship ceases when a horse-trade begins; but I am only taking you at your word."

"I sure done overlooked a bet, this trip," said Wishful. "Say, I reckon you must 'a' cut your first tooth on a cinch-ring. I done learnt somethin' this mornin'. Private eddication comes high, but I'm game. Write your check for a hundred—and take the bay. By rights I ought to give him to you, seein as how you done roped and branded me for a blattin' yearlin' the first throw; and you been out West just three days! You'll git along in this country."

"I hope so," laughed Bartley. "Speaking of getting along, I plan to visit Senator Brown. How long will it take me to get there, riding the bay?"

"He's got a runnin' walk that is good for six miles an hour. He's a walkin' fool. And anything you git your rope on, he'll hold it till you're gray-headed and got whiskers. That ole hoss is the best cow-hoss in Antelope County—and I'm referrin' you to Steve Brown to back me up. I bought that hoss from Steve. Any time you see the Box-S brand on a hoss, you can figure he's a good one."

"I suppose I'd have to camp on the mesa two or three nights," said Bartley.

"Nope! Ole Dobe'll make it in two days. He don't look fast, but the trail sure fades behind him when he's travelin'. I'm kind of glad you didn't try to buy the Antelope House. You'd started in pricin' the stable, and kind of milled around and ast me what I'd sell the kitchen for, and afore I knowed it, you'd 'a' had me selling the hotel for less than the stable. I figure you'd made a amazin' hand at shootin' craps."

"Let's step over and buy that saddle, and the rest of it. Will you engineer the deal? I don't know much about Western saddlery."

"Shucks! You can take that ole rig I was showin' you. She ain't much on looks, but she's all there."

"Thanks. But I'd rather buy a new outfit."

"When do you aim to start?"

"Right away. I suppose I'll need a blanket and some provisions."

"Yes. But you'll catch up with Cheyenne, if you keep movin'. He won't travel fast with a pack-hoss along. He'll most like camp at the first water, about twenty-five miles south. But you can pack some grub in your saddle-bags, and play safe. And take a canteen along."

Wishful superintended the purchasing of the new outfit, and

seemed unusually keen about seeing Bartley well provided for at the minimum cost. Wishful's respect for the Easterner had been greatly enhanced by the recent horse-deal. When it came to the question of clothing, Wishful wisely suggested overalls and a rowdy, as being weather and brush proof. Incidentally Wishful asked Bartley why he had paid his bill before he had actually prepared to start on the journey. Bartley told Wishful that he would not have prepared to start had he not paid the bill on impulse.

"Well, some folks git started on impulse, afore they pay their bills, and keep right on fannin' it," asserted Wishful.

An hour later Bartley was ready for the trail. With some food in the saddle-pockets, a blanket tied behind the cantle, and a small canteen hung on the horn, he felt equipped to make the journey. Wishful suggested that he stay until after the noon hour, but Bartley declined. He would eat a sandwich or two on the way.

"And ole Dobe knows the trail to Steve's ranch," said Wishful, as he walked around horse and rider, giving them a final inspection. "And you don't have to cinch ole Dobe extra tight," he advised. "He carries a saddle good. 'Course that new leather will stretch some."

"How old *is* Dobe?" queried Bartley. "You keep calling him 'old.'"

"I seen you mouthin' him, after you had saddled him. How old would *you* say?"

"Seven, going on eight."

"Git along! And if anybody gits the best of you in a hoss-trade, wire me collect. It'll sure be news!"

Bartley settled himself in the saddle and touched Dobe with the spurs.

"Give my regards to Senator Steve—and Cheyenne," called Wishful.

Wishful stood gazing after his recent guest until he had disappeared around a corner.

Then Wishful strode into the hotel office and marked a blue cross on the big wall calendar. A humorous smile played about his mouth. It was a mark to indicate the day and date that an Eastern tenderfoot had got the best of him in a horse-deal.

CHAPTER VII

AT THE WATER-HOLE

Before Bartley had been riding an hour he knew that he had a good horse under him. Dobe "followed his head" and did not flirt with his shadow, although he was grain-fed and ready to go. When Dobe trotted—an easy, swinging trot that ate into the miles—Bartley tried to post, English style. But Dobe did not understand that style of riding a trot. Each time Bartley raised in the stirrups, Dobe took it for a signal to lope. Finally Bartley caught the knack of leaning forward and riding a trot with a straight leg, and to his surprise he found it was a mighty satisfactory method and much easier than posting.

The mesa trail was wide—in reality a cross-country road, so Bartley had opportunity to try Dobe's different gaits. The running walk was a joy to experience, the trot was easy, and the lope as regular and smooth as the swing of a pendulum. Finally Bartley settled to the best long-distance gait of all, the running walk, and began to enjoy the vista; the wide-sweeping, southern reaches dotted with buttes, the line of the far hills crowded against the sky, and the intense light in which there was no faintest trace of blur or moisture. Everything within normal range of vision stood out clean-edged and definite.

Unaccustomed to riding a horse that neck-reined at the merest touch, and one that stopped at the slightest tightening of the rein, Bartley had to learn through experience that a spade bit requires delicate handling. He was jogging along easily when he turned to glance back at the town—now a far, huddled group of tiny buildings. Inadvertently he tightened rein. Dobe stopped short. Bartley promptly went over the fork and slid to the ground.

Dobe gazed down at his rider curiously, ears cocked forward, as though trying to understand just what his rider meant to do next. Bartley expected to see the horse whirl and leave for home. But Dobe stood patiently until his rider had mounted. Bartley glanced round covertly, wondering if any one had witnessed his impromptu descent. Then he laughed, realizing that it was a long way to Central Park, flat saddles and snaffles.

A little later he ate two of the sandwiches Wishful had thoughtfully provided, and drank from the canteen. Gradually the shadows of the buttes lengthened. The afternoon heat ebbed away in little, infrequent puffs of wind. The western reaches of the great mesa seemed to expand, while the southern horizon drew nearer.

Presently Bartley noticed pony tracks on the road, and either side of the tracks the mark of wheels. Here the wagon had swung aside to avoid a bit of bad going, yet the tracks of two horses still kept the middle of the road. "Senator Brown— and Cheyenne," thought Bartley, studying the tracks. He became interested in them. Here, again, Cheyenne had dismounted, possibly to tighten a cinch. There was the stub of a cigarette. Farther along the tracks were lost in the rocky ground of the petrified forest. He had made twenty miles without realizing it.

Winding in and out among the shattered and fallen trunks of those prehistoric trees, Bartley forgot where he was until he passed the bluish-gray sweep of burned earth edging the forest. Presently a few dwarf junipers appeared. He was getting higher, although the mesa seemed level. Again he discovered the tracks of the horses in the powdered red clay of the road.

He crossed a shallow arroyo, sandy and wide. Later he came suddenly upon a red clay cutbank, and a hint of water where the bank shadowed the mud-smeared rocks. He rode slowly, preoccupied in studying the country. The sun showed close to the rim of the world when he finally realized that, if he meant to get anywhere, he had better be about it. Dobe promptly caught the change of his rider's mental attitude and stepped out briskly. Bartley patted the horse's neck.

It was a pleasure to ride an animal that seemed to want to work with a man and not against him. The horse had cost one hundred dollars—a fair price for such a horse in those days. Yet Bartley thought it a very reasonable price. And he knew he had a bargain. He felt clearly confident that the big cow-pony would serve him in any circumstance or hazard.

As a long, undulating stretch of road appeared, softly brown in the shadows, Bartley began to look about for the water-hole which Wishful had spoken about. The sun slipped from sight. The dim, gray road reached on and on, shortening in perspective as the quick night swept down.

Beyond and about was a dusky wall through which loomed queer shapes that seemed to move and change until, approached, they became junipers. Bartley's gaze became fixed upon the road. That, at least, was a reality. He reached back and untied his coat and swung into it. An early star flared over the southern hills. He wondered if he had passed the water-hole. He had a canteen, but Dobe would need water. But Dobe was thoroughly familiar with the trail from Antelope to the White Hills. And Dobe smelled the presence of his kind, even while Bartley, peering ahead in the dusk, rode on, not aware that some one was camped within calling distance of the trail. A cluster of junipers hid the faint glow of the camp-fire.

Dobe stopped suddenly. Bartley urged him on. For the first time the big horse showed an inclination to ignore the rein. Bartley gazed round, saw nothing in particular, and spoke to the horse, urging him forward. Dobe turned and marched deliberately away from the road, heading toward the west, and nickered. From behind the screen of junipers came an answering nicker. Bartley hallooed. No one answered him. Yet Dobe seemed to know what he was about. He plodded on, down a slight grade. Suddenly the soft glow of a camp-fire illumined the hollow.

A blanket-roll, a saddle, a coil of rope, and a battered canteen and the fire—but no habitant of the camp.

"Hello!" shouted Bartley.

Dobe shied and snorted as a figure loomed in the dusk, and Cheyenne was peering up at him.

"Is this the water-hole?" Bartley asked inanely.

"This is her. I'm sure glad to see you! I feel like a plumb fool for standin' you up that way—but I didn't quite get you till I seen your face. I thought I knowed your voice, but I never did see you in jeans, and ridin' a hoss before. And that hat ain't like the one you wore in Antelope."

"Then you didn't know just what to expect?"

"I wa'n't sure. But say, I got some coffee goin'—and some bacon. Light down and give your saddle a rest."

"I'll just water my horse and stake him out and—"

"I'll show you where. I see you're ridin' Dobe. Wishful rent him to you?"

"No. I bought him."

"If you don't mind tellin' me—how much?"

"A hundred."

"Was Wishful drunk?"

"No."

"Well, you got a real hoss, there. The water is right close. Old Dobe knows where it is. Just lift off your saddle and turn him loose—or mebby you better hobble him the first night. He ain't used to travelin' with you, yet."

"I have a stake-rope," said Bartley.

"A hoss would starve on a stake-rope out here. I'll make you a pair of hobbles, pronto. Then he'll stick with my hosses."

"Where are they?"

"Runnin' around out there somewhere. They never stray far from camp."

Bartley watched Cheyenne untwist a piece of soft rope and make a pair of serviceable hobbles.

"Now he'll travel easy and git enough grass to keep him in shape. And them hobbles won't burn him. Any time you're shy of hobbles, that's how to make 'em."

Later, as Bartley sat by the fire and ate, Cheyenne asked him if Panhandle had been seen in town since the night of the crap game. Bartley told him that he had seen nothing of Panhandle.

"He's ridin' this country, somewhere," said Cheyenne. "You're headed for Steve's ranch?"

"Yes."

"Well, Steve'll sure give you the time of your life."

"I think I'll stay there a few days, if the Senator can make room for me."

"Room! Wait till you see Steve's place. And say, if you want to get wise to how they run a cattle outfit, just throw in with the boys, tell 'em you're a plumb tenderfoot and can't ride a bronc, nohow, and that you never took down a rope in your life, and that all you know about cattle is what you've et, and then the boys will use you white. There's nothin' puts a fella in wrong with the boys quicker than for him to let on he is a hand when he ain't. 'Course the boys won't mind seem' you top a bronc and get throwed, just to see if you got sand."

Meanwhile Cheyenne manipulated the coffee-pot and skillet most effectively. And while Bartley ate his supper, Cheyenne talked, seemingly glad to have a companion to talk to.

"You see," he began, apropos of nothing in particular, "entertainin' folks with the latest news is my long suit. I'm kind of a travelin' show, singin' and packin' the news around to everybody. 'Course folks read the paper and hear about somebody gettin' married, or gettin' shot or leavin' the country, and then they ask me the how of it. I been ramblin' so long that I know the pedigrees of 'most everybody down this way.

"Newspapers is all right, but folks get plumb hungry to git their news with human trimmin's. I recollec' I come mighty near gettin' in trouble, onct. Steve had some folks visitin' down to his ranch. They was new to the country, and seems they locked horns with a outfit runnin' sheep just south of Springerville. Now, I hadn't been down that way for about six months, but I had heard of that ruckus. So after Steve lets me sing a couple of songs, and I got to feelin' comfortable with them new folks, I set to and tells 'em about the ruckus down near Springerville. I guess the fella that told me must 'a' got his reins crossed, for pretty soon Steve starts to laugh and turns to them visitors and says: 'How about it, Mr. Smith?'

"Now, Smith was the fella that had the ruckus, and I'd been tellin' how that sheep outfit had run *him* out of the country. He was a young, long, spindlin' hombre from Texas—a reg'lar Whicker-bill, with that drawlin' kind of a voice that hosses and folks listen to. I knowed he was from Texas the minute I seen him, but I sure didn't know he was the man I was talkin' about.

"Everybody laughed but him and his wife. I reckon she was feelin' her oats, visitin' at the Senator's house. I don't know what she said to her husband, but, anyhow, afore I left for the bunk-house that evenin', he says, slow and easy, that if I was around there next mornin', he would explain all about that ruckus to me, when the ladies weren't present, so I wouldn't get it wrong, next time. I seen I had made a mistake for myself, and I didn't aim to make another, so I just kind of eased off and faded away, bushin' down that night a far piece from Senator Steve's ranch. I know them Whicker-bills and I didn't want to tangle with any of 'em."

"Afraid you'd get shot?" queried Bartley, laughing.

"Shot? Me? No, pardner. I was afraid that Texas gent would get shot. You see, he was married—and I—ain't."

Bartley lay back on his saddle and gazed up at the stars. The little fire had died down to a dot of red. A coyote yelped in the far dusk. Another coyote replied. Cheyenne rose and threw some wood on the fire. Then he stepped down to the water-hole and washed the plates and cups. Bartley could hear the peculiar thumping sound of hobbled horses moving about on the mesa. Cheyenne returned to the fire, picked up his bed-roll, and marched off into the bushes. Bartley wondered why he should take the trouble to move his bed-roll such a distance from the water-hole.

"Pack your saddle and blanket over, when you feel like turnin' in," said Cheyenne. "And you might throw some dirt on that fire. I ain't lookin' for visitors down this way, but you can't tell."

Bartley carried his saddle out to the distant clump of junipers.

"Just shed your coat and boots and turn in," invited Cheyenne.

Bartley was not sleepy, and for a long time he lay gazing up at the stars. Presently he heard Cheyenne snore. The Big Dipper grew dim. Then a coyote yelped—a shrill cadence of mocking laughter. "I wonder what the joke is?" Bartley thought drowsily.

Sometime during the night he was awakened by the tramping of horses, a sound that ran along the ground and diminished in the distance.

Cheyenne was sitting up. He touched Bartley. "Five or six of 'em," whispered Cheyenne.

"Our horses?"

"Too many. Mebby some strays."

"Or cowboys," suggested Bartley.

"Night-ridin' ain't so popular out here."

Bartley turned over and fell asleep. It seemed but a moment later that he was wide awake and Cheyenne was standing over him. It was daylight.

"They got our hosses," said Cheyenne.

"Who?"

"I dunno."

"What? *Our* horses? Great Scott, how far is it to Senator Brown's ranch?"

"About twenty-five miles, by road. I know a short cut."

Bartley jumped up and pulled on his boots. From the far hills came the faint yelp of a coyote, shrill and derisive.

"The joke is on us," said Bartley.

"This here ain't no joke," stated Cheyenne.

CHAPTER VIII

HIGH HEELS AND MOCCASINS

Bartley suggested that, perhaps, the horses had strayed.

Cheyenne shook his head. "My hosses ain't leavin' good feed, or leavin' me. They know this here country."

"Perhaps Dobe left for home and the rest followed him," said Bartley.

"Nope. Our hosses was roped and led south."

Bartley stared at Cheyenne, whose usually placid countenance expressed indecision and worry. Cheyenne seemed positive about the missing horses. Then Bartley saw an expression in Cheyenne's eyes that indicated more sternness of spirit than he had given Cheyenne credit for.

"Roped and led south," reiterated Cheyenne.

"How do you know it?"

"I been scoutin' around. The bunch that rode by last night was leadin' hosses. I could tell by the way the hosses was travelin'. They was goin' steady. If they'd been drivin' our hosses ahead, they would 'a' gone faster, tryin' to keep 'em from turnin' back. I don't see nothin' around camp to show who's been here."

"I'll make a fire," said Bartley.

"You got the right idea. We can eat. Then I aim to look around."

Cheyenne was over in the bushes rolling his bed when Bartley called to him, and he found Bartley pointing at a pair of dice on a flat rock beside the fire.

Cheyenne stooped and picked up the dice. "Was you rattlin' the bones to see if you could beat yourself?"

"I found them here. Are they yours?"

"Nope. And they weren't here last evenin'."

Cheyenne turned and strode out to the road while Bartley made breakfast. Cheyenne was gone a long time, examining the tracks of horses. When he returned he squatted down and ate.

Presently he rose. "First off, I thought they might 'a' been some stray Apaches or Cholas. But they don't pack dice. And the bunch that rode by last night was ridin' shod bosses."

Bartley turned slowly toward his companion. "Panhandle?" he queried.

"And these here dice? Looks like it. It's like him to leave them dice for us to play with while he trails south with our stack. I reckon it was that Dobe hoss he was after. But he must 'a' knowed who was campin' around here. You see, when Wishful kind of hinted to Panhandle to leave town, Panhandle figured that meant to stay out of Antelope quite a spell. First off he steals some hosses. Next thing, he'll sell 'em or trade 'em, down south of here. He'll travel nights, mostly."

"I can't see why he should especially pick us out as his victims," said Bartley.

"I don't say he did. But it would make no difference to him. He'd steal any man's stock. Only, I figure some of his friends must 'a' told him about you—that seen you ridin' down this way. He would know our camp would be somewhere near this water-hole. What kind of matches you got with you?"

"Why—this kind." And Bartley produced a few blue-top matches.

"This here is a old-timer sulphur match, cut square. It was right here, by the rock. Somebody lit a match and laid them dice there—sixes up. No reg'lar hoss-thief would take that much trouble to advertise himself. Panhandle done it—and he wanted me to know he done it."

"You've had trouble with him before, haven't you?"

"Yes—and no man can say I ever trailed him. But I never stepped out of his way."

"Then that crap game in Antelope meant more than an ordinary crap game?" said Bartley.

"He had his chance," stated Cheyenne.

"Well, we're in a fix," asserted Bartley.

Henry Herbert Knibbs

"Yes; we're afoot. But we'll make it. And right here I'm tellin' you that I aim to shoot a game of craps with Panhandle, usin' these here dice, that'll be fast and won't last long."

"How about the law?"

"The law is all right, in spots. But they's a whole lot of country between them spots."

Cheyenne cached the bed-roll, saddles, and cooking-outfit back in the brush, taking only a canteen and a little food. He proffered a pair of moccasins, parfleche-soled and comfortable, to Bartley.

"You wear these. Them new ridin'-boots'll sure kill you dead, walkin'. You can pack 'em along with you."

"How about your feet?"

"Say, you wouldn't call me a tenderfoot, would you?"

"Not exactly."

"Then slip on them moccasins. But first I aim to make a circle and see just where they caught up our stock."

Bartley drew on the moccasins and, tying his boots together, rolled them in his blanket. Meanwhile, Cheyenne circled the camp far out, examining the scattered tracks of horses. When he returned the morning sun was beginning to make itself felt.

"I'll toss up to see who wears the moccasins," said Bartley. "I'm more used to hiking than you are."

"Spin her!"

As Bartley tossed the coin, Cheyenne called. The half-dollar dropped and stuck edge-up in the sand.

"You wear 'em the first fifteen miles and then we'll swap," said Cheyenne.

Bartley filled the canteen and scraped dirt over the fire. Cheyenne took a last look around, and turned toward the south.

"You didn't say nothin' about headin' back to Antelope," said Cheyenne.

"Why, no. I started out to visit Senator Brown's ranch."

Cheyenne laughed. "Well, you're out to see the country, anyhow. We'll see lots, to-day."

Once more upon the road Cheyenne's manner changed. He seemed to ignore the fact that he was afoot, in country where there was little prospect of getting a lift from a passing rancher or freighter. And he said nothing about his horses, Filaree and Joshua, although Bartley knew that their loss must have hit him hard.

A mile down the road, and Cheyenne was singing his trail song, bow-legging ahead as though he were entirely alone and indifferent to the journey:

Seems like I don't git anywhere:
Git along, cayuse, git along!
But I'm leavin' here and I'm goin' there,
Git along, cayuse, git along—

He stopped suddenly, pulled his faded black Stetson over one eye, and then stepped out again, singing on:

They ain't no water and they ain't no shade:
They ain't no beer or lemonade,
But I reckon most like we'll make the grade
Git along, cayuse, git along.

"That's the stuff!" laughed Bartley. "A stanza or two of that every few miles, and we'll make the grade all right. That last was improvised, wasn't it?"

"Nope. Just naturalized. I make 'em up when I'm ridin' along, to kind of fit into the scenery. Impervisin' gets my wind."

"Well, if you are singing when we finish, you're a wonder," stated Bartley.

"Oh, I'm a wonder, all right! And mebby I don't feel like a plumb fool, footin' it into Steve's ranch with no hosses and no bed-roll and no reputation. And I sure lose mine this trip. Why, folks all over the country will josh me to death when they hear Panhandle Sears set me afoot on the big mesa. I reckon I'll have to kind of change my route till somethin' happens to make folks forget this here bobble."

Another five miles of hot and monotonous plodding, and Cheyenne stopped and sat down. He pulled off his boots.

Bartley offered the moccasins, but Cheyenne waved the offer aside.

"Just coolin' my feet," he explained. "It ain't so much the kind of boots, because these fit. It's scaldin' your feet that throws you."

They smoked and drank from the canteen. Five minutes' rest, and they were on the road again. The big mesa reached on and on toward the south, seemingly limitless, without sign of fence or civilization save for the narrow road that swung over each slight, rounded rise and ran away into the distance, narrowing to a gray line that disappeared in space.

Occasionally singing, Cheyenne strode along, Bartley striding beside him.

"You got a stride like a unbroke yearlin'," said; Cheyenne, as Bartley unconsciously drew ahead.

Bartley stopped and turned into step as Cheyenne caught up. He held himself to a slower pace, realizing that, while his companion could have outridden him by days and miles, the other was not used to walking.

As they topped a low rise a coyote sprang up and floated away. Bartley flinched as Cheyenne whipped up his gun and fired. The coyote jack-knifed and lay still. Cheyenne punched the empty shell from his gun, slipped in a cartridge, and strode on.

"Pretty fast work," remarked Bartley.

"Huh! I just throwed down on him to see if I was gettin' slow."

"It seems to me that if I could shoot like that, I wouldn't let any man back me down," said Bartley.

"Mebby so. But you're wrong, old-timer. Bein' fast with a gun is just like advertisin' for the coroner. Me, I'm plumb peaceful."

A few miles farther along they nooned in the shade of a pinion. When they started down the road again, Bartley noticed that Cheyenne limped slightly. But Cheyenne still refused to put on the moccasins. Bartley argued that his own feet were getting tender. He was unaccustomed to moccasins. Cheyenne turned this argument aside by singing a stanza of his trail song.

Also, incidentally, Cheyenne had been keeping his eye on the horse-tracks; and just before they left the main road taking a short cut, he pointed to them. "There's Filaree's tracks, and there's Joshua's. Your hoss has been travelin' over here, on the edge. Them hoss-thieves figure to hit into the White Hills and cut down through the Apache forest, most like."

"Will they sell the horses?"

"Yes. Or trade 'em for whiskey. Panhandle's got friends up in them hills."

"How far is it to the ranch?" queried Bartley.

"We done reached her. We're on Steve's ranch, right now. It's about five miles from that first fence over there to his house, by trail. It's fifteen by road."

"Then here is where you take the moccasins."

"Nope. My feet are so swelled you couldn't start my boots with a fence stretcher. They's no use both of us gettin' cripped up."

Bartley's own feet ached from the constant bruising of pebbles.

Presently Cheyenne dropped back and asked Bartley to set the pace.

"I'll just tie to your shadow," said Cheyenne. "Keeps me interested. When I'm drillin' along ahead I can't think of nothin' but my feet."

Because there was now no road and scarcely a trail, Bartley began to choose his footing, dodging the rougher places. The muscles of his calves ached under the unaccustomed strain of walking without heels. Cheyenne dogged along behind, suffering keenly from blistered feet, but centering his attention on Bartley's bobbing shadow. They had made about two miles across country when the faint trail ran round a butte and dipped into a shallow arroyo.

The arroyo deepened to a gulch, narrow and rocky. Up the gulch a few hundred yards they came suddenly upon a bunch of Hereford cattle headed by a magnificent bull. The trail ran in the bottom of the gulch. On either side the walls were steep and rocky. Angling junipers stuck out from the walls in occasional dots of green.

"That ole white-face sure looks hostile," Cheyenne remarked. "Git along, you ole Mormon; curl your tail and drift."

Cheyenne heaved a stone which took the bull fairly between the eyes. The bull shook his head and snapped his tail, but did not move. The cattle behind the bull stared blandly at the invaders of their domain. The bull, being an aristocrat, gave warning of his intent to charge by shaking his head and bellowing. Then he charged.

Cheyenne stooped for another stone, but Bartley had no intention of playing ping-pong with a roaring red avalanche. Bartley made for the side of the gulch and, catching hold of the bole of a juniper, drew himself up. Cheyenne stood to his guns, shied a third stone, scored a bull's-eye, and then decided to evacuate in favor of the enemy. His feet were sore, but he managed to keep a good three jumps ahead of the bull, up the precipitous bank of the gulch. There was no time to swing into the tree where Bartley had taken refuge, so Cheyenne backed into a shallow depression beneath the roots of the juniper.

The bull shook his head and butted at Cheyenne. Cheyenne slapped the bull's nose with his hat. The bull backed partway down the grade, snapped his tail, and bellowed. Up the grade he charged again. He could not quite reach Cheyenne, who slapped at the bull with his hat and spake eloquently.

Bartley, clinging to his precarious perch, gazed down upon the scene, wondering if he had not better take a shot at the bull. "Shall I let him have it?" he queried.

"Have what?" came the muffled voice of Cheyenne. "He's 'most got what he's after, right now."

"Shall I shoot him?"

"Hell, no! No use beefin' twelve hundred dollars' worth of meat. We don't need that much."

"Look out! He's coming again!" called Bartley.

Cheyenne had suddenly poked his head out of the shallow cave. The bull charged, backed down, and amused himself by tossing dirt over his shoulders and grumbling like distant thunder.

"Perhaps if you stay in that cave and don't show yourself, he'll leave," suggested Bartley.

"Stay nothin'!" answered Cheyenne. "There's a rattler in this here cave. I can hear him singin'. I'm comin' out, right now!"

Bartley leaned forward and glanced down. The branch on which he was straddled snapped.

"Look out below!" he shouted as he felt himself going.

Bartley's surprising evolution was too much for his majesty the bull, who whirled and galloped clumsily down the slope. Bartley rolled to the bottom, still holding to a broken branch of the tree. Cheyenne was also at the bottom of the gulch. The bull was trotting heavily toward his herd.

"Is there anything hooked to the back of my jeans?" queried Cheyenne.

"No. They're torn; that's all."

"Huh! I thought mebby that ole snake had hooked on to my jeans. He sounded right mad, singin' lively, back in there. My laigs feel kind of limp, right now."

Cheyenne felt of his torn overalls, shook his head, and then a slow smile illumined his face. "How do you like this here country, anyhow?"

"Great!" said Bartley.

CHAPTER IX

AT THE BOX-S

When they emerged from the western end of the gulch, they paused to rest. Not over a half-mile south stood the ranch-house, just back of a row of giant cottonwoods.

Cheyenne pointed out the stables, corrals, and bunk-house. "A mighty neat little outfit," he remarked, as they started on again.

"Little?"

"Senator Steve's only got about sixty thousand acres under fence."

"Then I'd like to see a big ranch," laughed Bartley.

"You can't. They ain't nothin' to see more'n you see right now. Why, I know a outfit down in Texas that would call this here ranch their north pasture—and they got three more about the same size, besides the regular range. But standin' in any one place you can't see any more than you do right now. Steve just keeps up this here ranch so he can have elbow-room. Yonder comes one of his boys. Reckon he seen us."

A rider had just reined his horse round and was loping toward them.

"He seen we was afoot," said Cheyenne.

"Mighty decent of him—" began Bartley, but Cheyenne waved the suggestion aside. "Decent nothin'! A man afoot looks as queer to a waddie as we did to that ole bull."

The puncher loped up, recognized Cheyenne, nodded to Bartley, and seemed to hesitate. Cheyenne made no explanation of their plight, so the puncher simply turned back and loped toward the ranch-house.

"Just steppin' over to tell Steve we're here," said Cheyenne, as Bartley's face expressed astonishment.

They plodded on, came to a gate, limped down a long lane, came to another gate, and there Senator Steve met them.

"I'd 'a' sent a man with a buckboard if I had known you planned to walk over from Antelope," he asserted, and his eyes twinkled.

Cheyenne frowned prodigiously. "Steve," he said slowly, "you can lovin'ly and trustfully go plumb to hell!"

Cheyenne turned and limped slowly toward the bunk-house.

Mrs. Brown welcomed Bartley as the Senator ushered him into the living-room. The Senator half-filled a tumbler from a cold, dark bottle and handed it to Bartley.

"'Green River,'" he said.

"Mrs. Brown," said Bartley as he bowed.

Then the Senator escorted Bartley to the bathroom. The tub was already filled with steaming water. A row of snow-white towels hung on the rack. The Senator waved his hand and, stepping out, closed the door.

A few minutes later he knocked at the bathroom door. "There's a spare razor in the cabinet, and all the fixings. And when you're ready there's a pair of clean socks on the doorknob."

Bartley heard the Senator's heavy, deliberate step as he passed down the hallway.

"A little 'Green River,' a hot bath, and clean socks," murmured Bartley. "Things might be worse."

His tired muscles relaxed under the beneficent warmth of the bath. He shaved, dressed, and stepped out into the hall. He sniffed. "Chicken!" he murmured soulfully.

Mrs. Senator Brown was supervising the cooking of a dinner that Bartley never forgot. Boiled chicken, dumplings, rich gravy, mashed potatoes, creamed carrots, sliced tomatoes— to begin with. And then the pie! Bartley furnished the appetite.

But that was not until after the Senator had returned from the bunk-house. He had seen to it that Cheyenne had had a bucket of hot water, soap, and towels and grease for his sore feet. In direct and effectual kindliness, without obviously expressed sympathy, the Westerner is peculiarly supreme.

Back in the living-room Bartley made himself comfortable, admiring the generous proportions of the house, the choice Indian blankets, the wide fireplace, and the general solidity of everything, which reflected the personality of his hosts.

Presently the Senator came in. "Cheyenne tells me that somebody set you afoot, down at the water-hole."

"Did he also tell you about your bull?"

"No! Is that how he came to tear his jeans?"

Bartley nodded. And he told the Senator of their recent experience in the gulch.

The Senator chuckled. "Don't say a word to Mrs. Brown about it. I'll have Cheyenne in, after dinner, and sweat it out of him. You see, Cheyenne won't eat with us. He always eats with the boys. No use asking him to eat in here. And, say, Bartley, we've got a little surprise for you. One of my boys caught up your horse, old Dobe. Dobe was dragging a rope. Looks like he broke away from some one. I had him turned into the corral. Dobe was raised on this range."

"Broke loose and came back!" exclaimed Bartley. "That's good news, Senator. I like that horse."

"But Cheyenne is out of luck," said the Senator. "He thought more of those horses, Filaree and Joshua, than he did of anything on earth. I'll send one of the boys back to the water-hole to-morrow, for your saddles and outfit. But now you're here, how do you like the country?"

"Almost as much as I like some of the people living in it," stated Bartley.

"Not including Panhandle Sears, eh?"

"I'm pretty well fed up on walking," and Bartley smiled.

"Sears is a worthless hombre," stated the Senator. "He's one of a gang that steal stock, and generally live by their wits and never seem to get caught. But he made a big mistake when he lifted Cheyenne's horses. Cheyenne already has a grievance against Sears. Some day Cheyenne will open up—and that will be the last of Mr. Sears."

"I had an idea there was something like that in the wind," said Bartley. "Cheyenne hasn't said much about Sears, but I was present at that crap game."

The Senator chuckled. "I heard about it. Heard you offered to take on Sears if he would put his gun on the table."

Bartley flushed. "I must have been excited."

The Senator leaned forward in his big, easy-chair. "Cheyenne wants me to let him take a couple of horses to trail Panhandle. And, judging from what Cheyenne said, he thinks you are going along with him. There's lots of country right round here to see, without taking any unnecessary risks."

"I understand," said Bartley.

"And this is your headquarters, as long as you want to stay," continued the Senator.

"Thank you. It's a big temptation to stay, Senator."

"How?"

"Well, it was rather understood, without anything being said, that I would help Cheyenne find his horses and mine. Dobe came back; but that hardly excuses me from going with Cheyenne."

"But your horse is here; and you seem to be in pretty fair

health, right now."

"I appreciate the hint, Senator."

"But you don't agree with me a whole lot."

"Well, not quite. Chance rather chucked us together, Cheyenne and me, and I think I'll travel with him for a while. I like to hear him sing."

"He likes to hear him sing!" scoffed the Senator, frowning. He sat back in his chair, blew smoke-rings, puffed out his cheeks, and presently rose. "Bartley, I see that you're set on chousin' around the country with that warbling waddie—just to hear him sing, as you say. I say you're a dam' fool.

"But you're the kind of a dam' fool I want to shake hands with. You aren't excited and you don't play to the gallery; so if there's anything you want on this ranch, from a posse to a pack-outfit, it's yours. And if either of you get Sears, I'll sure chip in my share to buy his headstone."

"I wouldn't have it inscribed until we get back," laughed Bartley.

"No; I don't think I will. Trailin' horse-thieves on their own stamping ground ain't what an insurance company would call a good risk."

Henry Herbert Knibbs

CHAPTER X

TO TRY HIM OUT

Two days later Cheyenne was able to get his feet into his boots, but even then he walked as though he did not care to let his left foot know what his right foot was doing. Lon Pelly, just in from a ride out to the line shack, remarked to the boys in the bunk-house that Cheyenne walked as though his brains were in his feet and he didn't want to get stone bruises stepping on them.

Cheyenne made no immediate retort, but later he delivered himself of a new stanza of his trail song, wherein the first line ended with "Pelly" followed by the rhymed assertion that the gentleman who bore that peculiar name had slivers in his anatomy due to a fondness for leaning against the bar of the Blue Front Saloon.

The boys were mightily pleased with the stanza, and they also improvised until, according to their versions, Long Lon bore a marked resemblance to a porcupine. Lon, being a real person, felt that Cheyenne's retaliation was just. Moreover, Lon, who never did anything hastily, let it be known casually that he had seen three riders west of the line shack some two days past, and that the riders were leading two horses, a buckskin and a gray. They were too far away to be distinguished absolutely, but he could tell the color of the horses.

"Panhandle?" queried a puncher.

"And two riders with him," said Long Lon.

"Goin' to trail him, Cheyenne?" came presently.

"That's me."

"Then let's pass the hat," suggested the first speaker.

"Wait!" said Cheyenne, drawing a pair of dice from his pocket. "Somehow, and sometime, I aim to shoot Panhandle a little game. Then you guys can pass the hat for the loser. Panhandle left them dice on the flat rock, by the water-hole. My pardner, Bartley, found them."

"Kind of sign talk that Pan pulled one on you," said Lon Pelly.

"He sure left his brains behind him when he left them dice," asserted Cheyenne. "I suspicioned that it was him—but the dice told me, plain."

"So you figure to walk up to Pan and invite him to shoot a little game, when you meet up with him?" queried a puncher.

"That's me."

"The tenderfoot"—he referred to Bartley—"is he goin' along with you?"

"He ain't so tender as you might think," said Cheyenne. "He's green, but not so dam' tender."

"Well, it's right sad. He looks like a pretty decent hombre."

"What's sad?" queried Cheyenne belligerently.

"Why, gettin' that tenderfoot all shot up, trailin' a couple of twenty-dollar cayuses. They ain't worth it."

"They ain't, eh?"

"Course, they make a right good audience, when you're singin'. They do all the listenin'," said another puncher.

"Huh! They ain't one of you got a hoss that can listen to you, without blushin'. You fellas think you're a hard-ridin'—"

"Ridin' beats walkin'," suggested Long Lon.

"Keep a-joshin'. I like it. Shows how much you don't know. I—hello, Mr. Bartley! Shake hands with Lon Pelly—but I guess you met him, over to Antelope. You needn't to mind the rest of these guys. They're harmless."

"I don't want to interrupt—" began Bartley.

"Set right in!" they invited in chorus. "We're just listenin' to Cheyenne preachin' his own funeral sermon."

Bartley seated himself in the doorway of the bunk-house. The joshing ceased. Cheyenne, who could never keep his hands still, toyed with the dice. Presently one of the boys suggested that Cheyenne show them some fancy work with a six-gun—"just to keep your wrist limber," he concluded.

Cheyenne shook his head. But, when Bartley intimated that he would like to see Cheyenne shoot, Cheyenne rose.

"All right. I'll shoot any fella here for ten bucks—him to name the target."

"No, you don't," said a puncher. "We ain't givin' our dough away, just to git rid of it."

"And right recent they was talkin' big," said Cheyenne. "I'll shoot the spot of a playin'-card, if you'll hold it," he asserted, indicating Bartley.

The boys glanced at Bartley and then lowered their eyes, wondering what the Easterner would do. Bartley felt that this was a test of his nerve, and, while he didn't like the idea of engaging in a William Tell performance he realized that Cheyenne must have had a reason for choosing him, out of the men present, and that Cheyenne knew his business.

"Cheyenne wants to git out of shootin'," suggested a puncher.

That settled it with Bartley. "He won't disappoint you," he stated quietly. "Give me the card."

One of the boys got up and fetched an old deck of cards. Bartley chose the ace of spades. Back of the corrals, with nothing but mesa in sight, he took up his position, while Cheyenne stepped off fifteen paces. Bartley's hand trembled a little. Cheyenne noticed it and turned to the group, saying something that made them laugh. Bartley's fingers tensed. He forgot his nervousness. Cheyenne whirled and shot, apparently without aim. Bartley drew a deep breath, and glanced at the card. The black pip was cut clean from the center.

"That's easy," asserted Cheyenne. Then he took a silver dollar from his pocket, laid it in the palm of his right hand, hung the gun, by its trigger guard on his right forefinger, lowered his hand and tossed the coin up. As the coin went up the gun whirled over. Then came the whiz of the coin as it cut through space.

"About seventy-five shots like that and I'm broke," laughed Cheyenne. "Anybody's hat need ventilatin'?"

"Not this child's," asserted Lon Pelly. "I sailed my hat for him onct. It was a twenty-dollar J.B., when I sailed it. When it hit it sure wouldn't hold water. Six holes in her—and three shots."

"Six?" exclaimed Bartley.

"The three shots went clean through both sides," said Lon.

Cheyenne reloaded his gun and dropped it into the holster.

Later, Bartley had a talk with Cheyenne about the proposed trailing of the stolen horses. Panhandle's name was mentioned. And the name of another man—Sneed. Cheyenne seemed to know just where he would look, and whom he might expect to meet.

Bartley and Cheyenne were in the living-room that evening talking with the Senator and his wife. Out in the bunk-house those of the boys who had not left for the line shack were discussing horse-thieves in general and Panhandle and Sneed in particular. Bill Smalley, a saturnine member of the outfit, who seldom said anything, and who was a good hand but a surly one, made a remark.

"That there Cheyenne is the fastest gun artist—and the biggest coward that ever come out of Wyoming. Ain't that right, Lon?"

"I never worked in Wyoming," said Long Lon.

CHAPTER XI

PONY TRACKS

Mrs. Senator Brown did not at all approve of Bartley's determination to accompany Cheyenne in search of the stolen horses. Late that night, long after Cheyenne had ceased to sing for the boys in the bunk-house, and while Bartley was peacefully slumbering in a comfortable bed, Mrs. Brown took the Senator to task for not having discouraged the young Easterner from attempting such a wild-goose chase. The Senator, whose diameter made the task of removing his boots rather difficult, puffed, and tugged at a tight riding-boot, but said nothing.

"Steve!"

"Yes'm. I 'most got it off. Wild-goose chase? Madam, the wild goose is a child that shuns this element. You mean wild-horse chase."

"That sort of talk may amuse your constituents, but you are talking to me."

Off came the stubborn boot. The Senator puffed, and tugged at the other boot.

Henry Herbert Knibbs

"No, ma'am. You're talking to me. There! Now go ahead and I'll listen."

"Why didn't you discourage Mr. Bartley's idea of making such a journey?'

"I did, Nelly. I told him he was a dam' fool."

Mrs. Senator Brown, who knew her husband's capabilities in dodging issues when he was cornered,—both at home and abroad,—peered at him over her glasses. "What else did you tell him?"

"Well, your honor," chuckled the Senator, "I also told him he was the kind of dam' fool I liked to shake hands with."

"I knew it! And what else?"

"I challenge the right of the attorney for the plaintiff to introduce any evidence that may—"

"The attorney for the defense may proceed," said Mrs. Brown, smiling.

"Why, shucks, Nelly! When you smile like that—why, I told Bartley he could have anything on this ranch that would help him get a rope on Sears."

"I knew it!"

"Then why did you ask me?"

Mrs. Brown ignored the question. "Very well, Stephen. Mr. Bartley gave me his sister's address, in case anything happened. She is his only living relative and I'm going to write to her at once and tell her what her brother is up to."

"And most like she'll head right for this ranch."

"Well, suppose she does? If she is anything like her brother she will be welcome."

"You bet! Just leave that to me!"

"It's a shame!" asserted Mrs. Brown.

"It is! With her good looks and inexperience she'll sure need somebody to look after her."

"How do you know she is good-looking?"

"I don't. I was just hoping."

"I shall write, just the same."

"I reckon you will. I'm going to bed."

Just as the sun rounded above the mesa next morning, Bartley stepped out to the veranda. He was surprised to find the Senator up and about, inspecting the details of Cheyenne's outfit, for Cheyenne had the horses saddled and packed. Bartley was still more surprised to find that Mrs. Brown had breakfast ready. Evidently the good Senator and his wife had a decided interest in the welfare of the expedition.

After breakfast the Senator's wife came out to the bunk-house with a mysterious parcel which she gave to Bartley. He sniffed at it.

"Cold chicken sandwiches!" he said, smiling broadly.

"And some doughnuts. It will save you boys fussing with a lunch."

Long Lon Pelly was also up and ready to start. The air was still cool and the horses were a bit snuffy. Lon mounted and rode toward the west gate where he waited for Cheyenne and Bartley.

"Now don't forget where you live," said the Senator as Bartley mounted.

With a cheery farewell to their hosts, Cheyenne and Bartley rode away. The first warmth of the sun touched them as they headed into the western spaces. Long Lon closed the big gate, stepped up on his horse, and jogged along beside them.

Bartley felt as though he had suddenly left the world of reality and was riding in a sort of morning dream. He could feel the pleasant warmth of the sun on his back. He sniffed the thin dust cast up by the horses. On either side of him the big mesa spread to the sky-line. Cattle were scattered in the brush, some of them lying down, some of them grazing indolently.

Presently Cheyenne began to sing, and his singing seemed to fit into the mood of the morning. He ceased, and nothing but the faint jingle of rein chains and the steady plod of hoofs disturbed the vast silence. A flicker of smoke drifted back as Cheyenne lighted a cigarette. Long Lon drilled on, wrapped in his reflections. Their moving shadows shortened. Occasionally a staring-eyed cow strayed directly in their way and stood until Long Lon struck his chaps with his quirt, when the cow, swinging its head, would whirl and bounce off to one side, stiff-legged and ridiculous.

Bartley unbuttoned his shirt-collar and pushed back his hat. Far across the mesa a dust devil spun up and writhed away toward the distant hills. As the horses slowed to cross a sandy draw, Bartley turned and glanced back. The ranch buildings—a dot of white in a clump of green—shimmered vaguely in the morning sunlight.

Thus far, Bartley felt that he had been leaving the ranch and the cheerful companionship of the Senator and his wife. But as Lon Pelly reined up—it was something like two hours since they had started—and pointed to a cross-trail leading south, Bartley's mental attitude changed instantly. Hitherto he had been leaving a pleasant habitation. Now he was going somewhere. He felt the distinction keenly. Cheyenne's verse came back to him.

> Seems like I don't git anywhere,
> Git along, cayuse, git along;
> But we're leavin' here and we're goin' there,
> Git along, cayuse, git along—

"Just drop a line when you get there," said Long Lon as he reined round and set off toward the far western sky-line. That was his casual farewell.

Cheyenne now turned directly toward the south and a range of hills that marked the boundary of the mesa level. Occasionally he got off his horse and stooped to examine tracks. Once he made a wide circle, leaving Bartley to haze the pack-horse along. Slowly they drew nearer to the hills. During the remainder of that forenoon, Cheyenne said nothing, but rode, slouched forward, his hand on the horn, his gaze on the ground.

They nooned in the foothills. The horses grazed along the edge of a tiny stream while Cheyenne and Bartley ate the cold chicken sandwiches. In half an hour they were riding again, skirting the foothills, and, it seemed to Bartley, simply meandering about the country, for now they were headed west again.

Henry Herbert Knibbs

Presently Cheyenne spoke. "I been makin' a plan."

"I didn't say a word," laughed Bartley.

"You didn't need to. I kind of got what you were thinkin'. This here is big country. When you're ridin' this kind of country with some fella, you can read his mind almost as good as a horse can. You was thinkin' I was kind of twisted and didn't know which way to head. Now take that there hoss, Joshua. Plenty times I've rode him up to a fork in the trail, and kep' sayin' to myself, 'We'll take the right-hand fork.' And Joshua always took the fork I was thinkin' about. You try it with Dobe, sometime."

"I have read of such things," said Bartley.

"Well, I *know* 'em. What would you say if I was to tell you that Joshua knowed once they was a fella ridin' behind me, five miles back, and out of sight—and told me, plain?"

"I wouldn't say anything."

"There's where you're wise. I can talk to you about such things. But when I try to talk to the boys like that, they just josh, till I git mad and quit. They ain't takin' me serious."

"What is your plan?" queried Bartley.

Cheyenne reined up and dismounted. "Step down, and take a look," he suggested.

Bartley dismounted. Cheyenne pointed out horse-tracks on the trail along the edge of the hills.

"Five hosses," he asserted. "Two of 'em is mine. That leaves three that are carryin' weight. But we're makin' a mistake for ourselves, trailin' Panhandle direct. He figures mebby I'd do that. I got to outfigure him. I don't want to git blowed out of my saddle by somebody in the brush, just waitin' for me to ride up and git shot. I got the way he's headed, and by tomorrow mornin' I'll know for sure.

"If he'd been goin' to swing back, to fool me, he'd 'a' done it before he hit the timber, up yonder. Once he gits in them hills he'll head straight south, for they ain't no other trail to ride on them ridges. But mebby he cut along the foothills, first. I got to make sure."

Late that afternoon and close to the edge of the foothills, Cheyenne lost the tracks. He spent over an hour finding them again. Bartley could discern nothing definite, even when Cheyenne pointed to a queer, blurred patch in some loose earth.

"It looks like the imprint of some coarse cloth," said Bartley.

"Gunnysack. They pulled the shoes off my hosses and sacked their feet."

"How about their own horses?"

"They been ridin' hard ground, and the tracks don't show, plain. Panhandle figured, when I seen that only the tracks of three horses showed, I'd think he had turned my hosses loose on the big mesa. He stops, pulls their shoes, sacks their feet, and leads 'em over there. Whoever done it was afoot, and steppin' careful. Hell, I could learn that yella-bellied hoss-thief how to steal hosses right, if I was in the business."

"Looks like a pretty stiff drill up those hills," remarked Bartley.

"That's why he turned, right here. 'Tain't just the stealin' of my hosses that's interestin' him. He's takin' trouble to run a whizzer on me—get me guessin'. Here is where we quit trailin' him. I got my plan workin' like a hen draggin' fence rails. We ain't goin' to trail Panhandle. We're goin' to ride 'round and meet him."

"Not a bad idea," said Bartley.

"It won't be—if I see him first."

CHAPTER XII

JIMMY AND THE LUGER GUN

Two days of riding toward the west, along the edge of the hills, and Bartley and Cheyenne found themselves approaching the high country. The trail ran up a wide valley, on either side of which were occasional ranches reaching back toward the slopes. In reality they were gradually climbing the range on an easy grade and making good time.

Their course now paralleled the theoretical course of Panhandle and his fellows. Dodging the rugged land to the south, Cheyenne had swung round in a half-circle, hoping to head off Panhandle on the desert side of the range. Since abandoning the tracks of the stolen horses, Cheyenne had resumed his old habit of singing as he rode. He seemed to know the name of every ranch, and of every person they met.

Once or twice some acquaintance expressed surprise that Cheyenne did not stop and spend the night with him. But Cheyenne jokingly declined all invitations, explaining to Bartley that in stopping to visit they would necessarily waste hours in observing the formalities of arrival and departure, although Cheyenne did not put it just that way.

They found water and plenty of feed, made their camps

early, broke camp early, and rode steadily. With no visible incentive to keep going, Bartley lost his first keen interest in the hunt, and contented himself with listening to Cheyenne's yarns about the country and its folk, or occasionally chatting with some wayfarer. But never once did Cheyenne hint, to those they met, just why he was riding south.

There were hours at a stretch, when the going was level, when Cheyenne did nothing but roll his gun, throw down on different objects, toss up his gun, and catch it by the handle; and once he startled Bartley by making a quick fall from the saddle and shooting from the ground. Cheyenne explained to Bartley that often, when riding alone, he had spent hour after hour figuring out the possibilities of gun-play, till it became evident to the Easterner that, aside from being naturally quick, there was a very good reason for Cheyenne's proficiency with the six-gun. He practiced continually. And yet, thought Bartley, one of the Box-S punchers had said that Cheyenne had never killed anything bigger than a coyote, and never would—intimating that he was too good-natured ever to take advantage of his own proficiency with a gun.

Bartley wondered just how things would break if they did happen to meet Panhandle unexpectedly. Panhandle would no doubt dispose of the stolen horses as soon as he could. What excuse would Cheyenne have to call Panhandle to account? And when it came to a show-down, *would* Cheyenne call him to account?

Bartley was thinking of this when they made an early camp, the afternoon of the third day out. After the horses were hobbled and the packs arranged, Bartley decided to experiment a little with his new Luger automatic. Cheyenne declined to experiment with the gun.

"It's a mean gat," he asserted, "and it's fast. But I'll bet you a new hat I can empty my old smoke-wagon quicker than you can that pocket machine gun."

For the fun of the thing, Bartley took him up. He selected as target a juniper stump, and blazed away.

"I'm leavin' the decision to you," said Cheyenne, as he braced his right arm against his body and fanned the Colt, emptying it before Bartley could realize that he had fired three shots—and Cheyenne had fired five.

"I'll buy you that hat when we get to town," laughed Bartley. "You beat me, hands down."

"Hands down is right, old-timer. Fannin' a gun is show stuff, but it's wicked, at close range."

Meanwhile, Bartley had been experimenting further with the Luger. When he got through he had a hat full of pieces and Cheyenne was staring at what seemed to be the wreck of a once potent weapon.

"Why, you done pulled that little lead sprinkler all to bits!" exclaimed Cheyenne, "and you didn't have no tools to do it with."

"You can take down and assemble this gun without tools," stated Bartley. "All you need is your fingers."

"But what in Sam Hill did you pull her apart for?"

"Just to see if I could put her together again."

Cheyenne scratched his head, and stepped over to inspect the juniper stump. He stooped, whistled, and turned to Bartley. "Man, you like to sawed that stub in two. Why didn't you say you could shoot?"

"I can't, in your class. But tell me why you Westerners always seem to think it strange that an Easterner can sit a horse or shoot fairly well? Is it because you consider that the average tourist represents the entire East?"

"I dunno. But, then, I've met up with Easterners that weren't just like you."

Bartley was busy, assembling the Luger, and Cheyenne was watching him, when they glanced up simultaneously. A shadow drifted between them.

Cheyenne hesitated and then stepped forward. "I'll be dinged if it ain't Jimmy! What you doin' up here in the brush, anyhow?"

The boy, who rode a well-mannered gray pony, kicked one foot out of the stirrup and hooked his small leg over the horn. He nodded to Cheyenne, but his interest was centered on Bartley and the Luger.

"It's Jimmy—my boy," said Cheyenne. "His Aunt Jane lives over yonder, a piece."

"Why, hello!" exclaimed Bartley, laying the pistol aside. And he stepped up and shook hands with the boy, who grinned.

"How's the folks?" queried Cheyenne.

"All right. That there is a Luger gun, ain't it?"

"Yes," said Bartley. "Would you like to try it?"

The boy scrambled down from the saddle. "Honest?"

"Ain't you goin' to say hello to your dad?" queried Cheyenne.

"Sure! Only I was lookin' at that Luger gun—"

Jimmy shook hands perfunctorily with his father and turned to Bartley, expectancy in his gaze.

Bartley reloaded the gun and handed it to the boy, who straightaway selected the juniper stump and blazed away. Bartley watched him, a sturdy youngster, brown-fisted, blue-eyed, with sandy hair, and dressed in jeans and a rowdy—a miniature cow-puncher, even to his walk.

"Ever shoot one before?" queried Bartley as the boy gave back the pistol.

"Nope. There's one like it, over to the store in San Andreas. It's in the window. I never got to look at it right close."

"Try it again," said Bartley.

The boy grinned. "I reckon you're rich?"

"Why?"

"'Cause you got a heap of ca'tridges. They cost money."

"Never mind. Go ahead and shoot."

Jimmy blazed away again and ran to see where his bullets had hit the stump. "She's a pretty fair gun," he said as he handed it back. "But I reckon I'll have to stick to my ole twenty-two rifle. She's gettin' wore out, but I can hit things with her, yet. I git rabbits."

Henry Herbert Knibbs

"Now, mebby you got time to tell us something about Aunt Jane and Uncle Frank and Dorry," suggested Cheyenne.

"Why, they're all right," said the boy. "Why didn't you stop by to our place instead of bushin' way up here?"

Cheyenne hesitated. "I reckon I'll be comin' over," he said finally.

Bartley put the Luger away. The boy turned to his father. Cheyenne's face expressed happiness, yet Bartley was puzzled. The boy was not what could be termed indifferent in any sense, yet he had taken his father's presence casually, showing no special interest in their meeting. And why had Cheyenne never mentioned the boy? Bartley surmised that there was some good reason for Cheyenne's silence on that subject—and because it was obvious that there was a good reason, Bartley accepted the youngster's presence in a matter-of-fact manner, as though he had known all along that Cheyenne had a son. In fact, Cheyenne had not stopped to think about it at all. If he had, he would have reasoned that Bartley had heard about it. Almost every one in Arizona knew that Cheyenne had been married and had separated from his wife.

"That would be a pretty good gun to git hoss-thieves with," asserted the boy, still thinking of the Luger.

"What do you know about hoss-thieves?" queried Cheyenne.

"You think I didn't see you was ridin' different hosses!" said Jimmy. "Mebby you think I don't know where Josh and Filaree are."

"You quit joshin' your dad," said Cheyenne.

"I ain't joshin' *nobody*. Ole 'Clubfoot' Sneed, over by the re'savation's got Josh and Filaree. I seen 'em in his corral, yesterday. I was up there, huntin'."

"Did you talk to him?" queried Cheyenne.

"Nope. He just come out of his cabin an' told me to fan it. I wasn't doin' nothin'. He said it was against the law to be huntin' up there. Mebby he don't hunt when he feels like it!"

"Did you tell Uncle Frank?"

"Yep. Wish I hadn't. He says for me to stay away from the high country—and not to ride by Sneed's place any more."

Cheyenne turned to Bartley. "I done made one guess right," he said.

"You goin' to kill Sneed?" queried young Jim enthusiastically.

"Nobody's goin' to get killed. But I aim to git my hosses."

Cheyenne turned to Jimmy. "You ride over and tell Uncle Frank and Aunt Jane that me and Mr. Bartley'll be over after we eat."

"Will you sing that 'Git Along' song for me, dad?"

"You bet!"

"But why don't you come over and eat to our place? You always stop by, every time you ride down this way," said Jimmy.

"You ride right along, like I told you, or you'll be late for your supper."

Little Jim climbed into the saddle, and, turning to cast a lingering and hopeful glance at Bartley,—a glance which suggested the possibilities of further practice with the Luger gun,—he rode away, a manful figure, despite his size.

"They're bringin' my kid up right," said Cheyenne, as though in explanation of something about which he did not care to talk.

CHAPTER XIII

AT AUNT JANE'S

Aunt Jane Lawrence was popular with the young folks of the district, not alone because she was a good cook, but because she was a sort of foster mother to the entire community. The young ladies of the community brought to Aunt Jane their old hats and dresses, along with their love affairs, petty quarrels, and youthful longings. A clever woman at needlework, she was often able to remodel the hats and "turn" the dresses so that they would serve a second season or maybe a third.

The love affairs, petty quarrels, and youthful longings were not always so easy to remodel, even when they needed it: but Aunt Jane managed well. She had much patience and sympathy. She knew the community, and so was often able to help her young friends without conflicting with paternal or maternal views. Hat-trimming and dressmaking were really only incidental to her real purpose in life, which was to help young folks realize their ideals, when such ideals did not lead too far from everyday responsibilities.

Yet, with all her capabilities, her gentle wisdom, and her unobtrusive sympathy, she was unable to influence her Brother Jim—known by every one as "Cheyenne"—toward a settled habit of life. So it became her fondest desire to see that Cheyenne's boy, Little Jim, should be brought up in a home that he would always cherish and respect. Aunt Jane's husband Frank Lawrence, had no patience with Cheyenne's aimless meanderings. Frank Lawrence was a hard-working, silent nonentity. Aunt Jane was the real manager of the ranch, and incidentally of Little Jim, and her husband was more than content that it should be so.

Occasionally Aunt Jane gave a dance at her home. The young folks of the valley came, had a jolly time, and departed, some of them on horseback, some in buckboards, and one or two of the more well-to-do in that small but aggressive vehicle which has since become a universal odor in the nostrils of the world.

Little Jim detested these functions which entailed his best clothes and his best behavior. He did not like girls, and looked down with scorn upon young men who showed any preference for the sex feminine. He made but two exceptions to this hard-baked rule: his Aunt Jane, and her young friend who lived on the neighboring ranch, Dorothy. Little Jim called her Dorry because it sounded like a boy's name. And he liked Dorry because she could ride, and shoot with a twenty-two rifle almost as well as he could. Then, she didn't have a beau, which was the main thing. Once he told her frankly that if she ever got a beau, he—Jimmy—was going to quit.

"Quit what?" asked Dorothy, smiling.

Little Jim did not know just what he was going to quit, but he had imagination.

"Why, quit takin' you out huntin' and campin' and showin' you how to tell deer tracks from goat's tracks—and everything."

"But I have a beau," said Dorothy teasingly.

"Who is he?" demanded Little Jim.

"Promise you won't tell?"

Little Jim hesitated. He did not consider it quite the thing to promise a girl anything. But he was curious. "Uh-huh," he said.

"Jimmy Hastings!" said Dorothy, laughing at his expression.

"That ain't fair!" blurted Little Jim. "I ain't nobody's beau. Shucks! Now you gone and spoiled all the fun."

"I was only teasing you, Jimmy." And she patted Little Jim's tousled head. He wriggled away and smoothed down his hair.

"I can beat you shootin' at tin cans," he said suddenly, to change the subject.

Shooting at tin cans was much more interesting than talking about beaux.

"I have to help Aunt Jane get supper," said Dorothy, who had been invited to stay for supper that evening. In fact, she was often at the Hastings ranch, a more than welcome guest.

Jimmy scowled. Dorry was always helping Aunt Jane make dresses or trim hats, or get supper. A few minutes later Little Jim was out back of the barn, scowling over the sights of his twenty-two at a tomato can a few yards away. He fired and punctured the can.

"Plumb center!" he exclaimed. "You think you're her beau,

do you? Well, that's what you get. And if I see you around this here ranch, just even *lookin'* at her, I'll plug you again." Jimmy was romancing, with the recently discussed subject of beaux in mind.

When Little Jim informed the household that his father and another man were coming over, that evening, Uncle Frank asked who the other man was. Little Jim described Bartley and told about the wonderful Luger gun.

"My dad is huntin' his hosses," he said. "And I know who's got 'em!"

"Was the other man a deputy?" queried Uncle Frank.

"He didn't have a badge on him. He kind of acted like everything was a joke—shootin' at that stump, and everything. He wasn't mad at nobody. And he looked kind of like a dude."

Little Jim meanwhile amused himself by trying to rope the family cat with a piece of clothesline. Uncle Frank, who took everything seriously, asked Little Jim if he had told his father where the horses were.

"Sure I told him. Wouldn't you? They're dad's hosses, Filaree and Josh. I guess he'll make ole Clubfoot Sneed give 'em back!"

"You want to be careful what you say about Mr. Sneed, Jimmy. And don't you go to ridin' over that way again. We aim to keep out of trouble."

Little Jim had succeeded in noosing the cat's neck. That sadly molested animal jumped, rolled over, and clawed at the rope, and left hurriedly with the bit of clothesline trailing in its wake.

"I got to git that cat afore he hangs himself," stated Little Jim, diving out of the house and heading for the barn. Thus he avoided acknowledging his uncle's command to stay away from Sneed's place.

Supper was over and the dishes were washed and put away when Cheyenne and Bartley appeared. Clean-shaven, his dark hair brushed smoothly, a small, dark-blue, silk muffler knotted loosely about his throat, and in a new flannel shirt and whipcord riding-breeches—which he wore under his jeans when on the trail—Bartley pretty well approximated Little Jim's description of him as a dude. And the word "dude" was commonly used rather to differentiate an outlander from a native than in an exactly scornful sense. Without a vestige of self-consciousness, Bartley made himself felt as a distinct entity, physically fit and mentally alert. Cheyenne, with his cow-puncher gait and his general happy-go-lucky attitude, furnished a strong contrast to the trim and well-poised Easterner. Dorothy was quick to appreciate this. She thought that she rather liked Bartley. He was different from the young men whom she knew. Bartley was pleased with her direct and natural manner of answering his many questions about Western life.

Presently he found himself talking about his old home in Kentucky, and the thorough-bred horses of the Blue Grass. The conversation drifted to books and plays, but never once did it approach the subject of guns—and Little Jim, who had hoped that the subject of horse-thieves might be broached, felt altogether out of the running.

He waited patiently, for a while. Then during a lull in the talk he mentioned Sneed's name.

Henry Herbert Knibbs

"Jimmy!" reprimanded his Uncle Frank.

"Yes, sir?"

Uncle Frank merely gestured, significantly.

Little Jim subsided, frowning, and making a face at Dorothy, who was smiling at him. It seemed mighty queer that, when *he* "horned in," his Aunt Jane or his uncle always said "Jimmy!" in that particular tone. But when any of the grown-ups interrupted, no one said a word. However, Bartley was not blind to Little Jim's attitude of forced silence, and presently Bartley mentioned the subject of guns, much to Little Jim's joy. Little Jim worked round to the subject of twenty-two rifles, intimating that his own single-shot rifle was about worn out.

Uncle Frank heard and promptly changed the subject. Little Jim was disgusted. A boy just wouldn't talk when other folks were talking, and he couldn't talk when they were not. What was the use of living, anyhow, if you had to go around without talking at all, except when somebody asked you if you had forgotten to close the lane gate and had let the stock get into the alfalfa—and you had to say that you had?

However, Little Jim had his revenge. When Aunt Jane proffered apple pie, later in the evening, Jimmy prefixed his demand for a second piece with the statement that he knew there was another uncut pie in the kitchen, because Aunt Jane had said maybe his dad would eat half a one, and then ask for more.

This gentle insinuation brought forth a sharp reprimand from Uncle Frank. But Jimmy had looked before he leaped.

"Well, Aunt Jane said so. Didn't you, Aunt Jane?"

Whereat every one laughed, including the gentle Aunt Jane. And Jimmy got his second piece of pie.

After the company had found itself, Uncle Frank, Cheyenne, and Bartley forgathered out on the veranda and talked about the missing horses. Little Jim sat silently on the steps, hoping that the talk would swing round to where he could have his say. If he had not discovered the missing horses, how would his father know where they were? It did not seem exactly fair to Little Jim that he should be ignored in the matter.

"I'd just ride over and talk with Sneed," suggested Uncle Frank.

"Oh, I'll do that, all right," asserted Cheyenne.

"But I'd go slow. You might talk like your stock had strayed and you were looking for them. Sneed and Panhandle Sears are pretty thick. I'd start easy, if I was in your boots."

This from the cautious Uncle Frank.

"But you'd go get 'em, if they happened to be your hosses," said Cheyenne. "You're always tellin' me to step light and go slow. I reckon you expect me to sing and laugh and josh and take all the grief that's comin' and forget it."

"No," said Uncle Frank deliberately. "If they was my hosses, I'd ride over and get 'em. But I can't step into your tangle. If I did, Sneed would just nacherally burn us out, some night. There's only two ways to handle a man like Clubfoot Sneed: one is to kill him, and the other is to leave him alone. And it's got to be one or the other when you live as close to the hills as we do. I aim to leave him alone, unless he tries to ride me."

"Which means that you kind of think I ought to let the hosses go, for fear of gettin' you in bad."

Uncle Frank shook his head, but said nothing. Bartley smoked a cigar and listened to the conversation that followed. Called upon by Uncle Frank for his opinion, Bartley hesitated, and then said that, if the horses were his, he would be tempted to go and get them, regardless of consequences. Bartley's stock went up, with Little Jim, right there.

Cheyenne turned to Uncle Frank. "I'm ridin' over to Clubfoot's wikiup to-morrow mornin'. I'll git my hosses, or git him. And I'm ridin' alone."

Little Jim, meanwhile, had been raking his mind for an idea as to how he might attract attention. He disappeared. Presently he appeared in front of the veranda with the end of a long rope in his fist. He blinked and grinned.

"What's on the other end of that rope?" queried Uncle Frank, immediately suspicious.

"Nothin' but High-Tail."

"I thought I told you not to rope that calf," said Uncle Frank, rising.

"I didn't. I jest held my loop in front of some carrots and High-Tail shoves his head into it. Then I says, 'Whoosh!' and he jumps back—and I hung on."

"How in Sam Hill did you get him here?" queried Uncle Frank.

"Jest held a carrot to his nose—and he walked along tryin' to get it."

"Well you shake off that loop and haze him back into the corral."

High-Tail, having eaten the carrot, decided to go elsewhere. He backed away and blatted. Little Jim took a quick dally round a veranda post. High-Tail plunged and fought the rope.

"Turn him loose!" cried Uncle Frank.

"What's the matter?" said Aunt Jane, appearing in the doorway.

Little Jim eased off the dally, but clung to the rope. High-Tail whirled and started for the corral. Little Jim set back on his heels, but Little Jim was a mere item in High-Tail's wild career toward freedom. A patter of hoofs in the dark, and Little Jim and the calf disappeared around the corner of the barn.

Cheyenne laughed and rose, following Uncle Frank to the corral. When they arrived, High-Tail had made his third round of the corral, with Jimmy still attached to the rope. Cheyenne managed to stop the calf and throw off the noose.

Little Jim rose and gazed wildly around. He was one color, from head to foot—and it was a decidedly local color. His jeans were torn and his cotton shirt was in rags, but his grit was unsifted.

"D-didn't I hang to him, dad?" he inquired enthusiastically.

"You sure did!" said Cheyenne.

With a pail of hot water, soap, and fresh raiment, Aunt Jane undertook to make Little Jim's return to the heart of the family as agreeable as possible to all concerned.

Henry Herbert Knibbs

"Isn't he hurt?" queried Bartley.

"Not if he doesn't know it," stated Cheyenne.

CHAPTER XIV

ANOTHER GAME

Cheyenne knew enough about Sneed, by reputation, to make him cautious. He decided to play ace for ace—and, if possible, steal the stolen horses from Sneed. The difficulty was to locate them without being seen. Little Jim had said the horses were in Sneed's corral, somewhere up in the mountain meadows. And because Cheyenne knew little about that particular section of the mountains, he rolled a blanket and packed some provisions to see him through. Bartley and he had returned to their camp after their visit to the ranch, and next morning, as Cheyenne made preparation to ride, Bartley offered to go with him.

Cheyenne dissuaded Bartley from accompanying him, arguing that he could travel faster and more cautiously alone. "One man ridin' in to Sneed's camp wouldn't look as suspicious as two," said Cheyenne. "And if I thought you could help any, I'd say to come along. That's on the square. Me and my little old carbine will make out, I guess."

So Bartley, somewhat against his inclination, stayed in camp, with the understanding that, if Cheyenne did not return in two days, he was to report the circumstance to the authorities in San Andreas, the principal town of the valley.

Meanwhile, the regular routine prevailed at the Lawrence ranch. Uncle Frank had the irrigation plant to look after; and Aunt Jane was immersed in the endless occupation of housekeeping. Little Jim had his regular light tasks to attend to, and that morning he made short work of them. It was not until noon that Aunt Jane missed him. He had disappeared completely, as had his saddle-pony.

At first, Jimmy had thought of riding over to his father's camp, but he was afraid his father would guess his intent and send him back home. So he tied his pony to a clump of junipers some distance from the camp, and, crawling to a rise, he lay and watched Cheyenne saddle up and take the trail that led into the high country. A half-hour later, Jimmy mounted his pony and, riding wide of the camp, he cut into the hill trail and followed it on up through the brush to the hillside timber. He planned to ride until he got so far into the mountains that when he did overtake his father and offer his assistance in locating the stolen horses, it would hardly seem worth while to send him back. Jimmy expected to be ordered back, but he had his own argument ready in that event.

Little Jim's pony carried him swiftly up the grade. Meanwhile, Cheyenne had traveled rather slowly, saving his horse. At a bend in the trail he drew rein to breathe the animal. On the lookout for any moving thing, he glanced back and down—and saw an old black hat bobbing along through the brush below. He leaned forward and peered down. "The little cuss!" he exclaimed, grinning. Then his expression changed. "Won't do, a-tall! His aunt will be havin' fits—and Miss Dorry'll be helpin' her to have 'em, if she hears of it. Dog-gone that boy!"

Nevertheless, Cheyenne was pleased. His boy had sand, and liked adventure. Little Jim might have stayed in camp, with Bartley, and spent a joyous day shooting at a mark, incidentally hinting to the Easterner that "his ole twenty-two was about worn out." But Little Jim had chosen to follow his father into the hills.

"Reckon he figures to see what'll happen," muttered Cheyenne as he led his horse off the trail and waited for Jimmy to come up.

Little Jim's black hat bobbed steadily up the switchbacks. Presently he was on the stretch of trail at the end of which his father waited, concealed in the brush.

As Little Jim's pony approached the bend it pricked its ears and snorted. "Git along, you!" said Jimmy.

"Where you goin'?" queried Cheyenne, stepping out on the trail.

Little Jim gazed blankly at his father. "I'm just a-ridin'. I wa'n't goin' no place."

"Well, you took the wrong trail to get there. You fan it back to the folks."

"Aunt Jane is my boss!" said Jimmy defiantly. "'Course she is," agreed Cheyenne. "You and me, we're just pardners. But, honest, Jimmy, you can't do no good, doggin' along after me. Your Aunt Jane would sure stretch my hide if she knowed I let you come along."

"I won't tell her."

"But she'd find out. You just ride back and wait down at my camp. I'll find them hosses, all right."

Little Jim hesitated, twisting his fingers in his pony's mane.

"Suppose," he ventured, "that a bunch of Sneed's riders was to run on to you? You'd sure need help."

"That's just it! Supposin' they did? And supposin' they took a crack at us, they might git you—for you sure look man-size, a little piece off."

Jimmy grinned at the compliment, but compliments could not alter his purpose. "I got my ole twenty-two loaded," he asserted hopefully.

"Then you just ride back and help Mr. Bartley take care of the hosses. He ain't much of a hand with stock."

"Can't I go with you?"

"Not this trip, son. But I'll tell you somethin'. Mr. Bartley, down there, said to me this mornin' that he was goin' to buy you a brand-new twenty-two rifle, one of these days: mebby after we locate the hosses. You better have a talk with him about it."

This *was* a temptation to ride back: yet Jimmy had set his heart on going with his father. And his father had said that he was simply going to ride up to Sneed's place and have a talk with him. Jimmy wanted to hear that talk. He knew that his father meant business when he had told him to go back.

"All right for you!" said Jimmy finally. And he reined his pony round and rode back down the trail sullenly, his black hat pulled over his eyes, and his small back very straight and stiff.

Cheyenne watched him until the brush of the lower levels intervened. Then Cheyenne began the ascent, his eye alert, his mind upon the task ahead. When Little Jim realized that his father was so far into the timber that the trail below was shut from view, he reined his pony round again and began to climb the grade, slowly, this time, for fear that he might overtake his father too soon.

Riding the soundless upland trail that meandered among the spruce and pine, skirting the edges of the mountain meadows and keeping within the timber, Cheyenne finally reached the main ridge of the range. Occasionally he dismounted and examined the tracks of horses.

It was evident that Sneed had quite a bunch of horses running in the meadows. Presently Cheyenne came to a narrow trail which crossed a meadow. At the far end of the trail, close to the timber, was a spring, fenced with poles. The spring itself was boxed, and roundabout were the marks of high-heeled boots. Cheyenne realized that he must be close to Sneed's cabin. He wondered if he had been seen.

If he had, the only thing to do was to act natural. He was now too close to a habitation—although he could see none—to do otherwise. So he dismounted and, tying his horse to the spring fence, he stepped through the gate and picked up the rusted tin cup and dipped it in the cold mountain water. He had the cup halfway to his lips when his horse nickered. From somewhere in the brush came an answering nicker. Cheyenne, kneeling, threw the water from the cup as though he had discovered dirt in it, and dipped the cup again.

Behind him he heard his horse moving restlessly. As Cheyenne raised the cup to drink, he half closed his eyes, and glancing sideways, caught a glimpse of a figure standing near the upper end of the spring fence. Cheyenne drank, set down the cup, and, rising, turned his back on the figure, and, stretching his arms, yawned heartily. He strode to his horse, untied the reins, mounted, and began to sing:

Seems like I don't get anywhere
Git along, cayuse, git along!
But we're leavin' here and—

"What's your hurry?" came from behind him.

Cheyenne turned and glanced back. "Hello, neighbor! Now, if I'd 'a' knowed you was around, I'd 'a' asked you to have a drink with me."

A tall, heavy-set mountain man, bearded, and limping noticeably, stepped round the end of the spring fence and strode toward him. From Uncle Frank's description, Cheyenne at once recognized the stranger as Sneed. Across Sneed's left arm lay a rifle. Cheyenne saw him let down the hammer as he drew near.

"Where you headed?" queried Sneed.

"Me, I'm lookin' for Bill Sneed's cabin. You ain't Sneed, are you?"

"Yes, I'm Sneed."

"Well, I'm in luck. I'm Cheyenne Hastings."

"That don't buy you nothin' around here. What do you want to see me about?"

"Why, I done lost a couple of hosses the other night. I reckon somethin' stampeded 'em, for they never strayed far from camp before. I trailed 'em up to the hills and then lost their tracks on the rocks. Thought I'd ride up and see if you had seen 'em—a little ole buckskin and a gray."

Sneed waved his hand toward the east. "My corrals are over

there. You're welcome to look my stock over."

"Thanks. This way, you said?"

"Straight ahead."

Cheyenne hesitated, hoping that Sneed would take the lead. But the mountain man merely gestured again and followed Cheyenne through a patch of timber, and across another meadow—and Cheyenne caught a glimpse of the ridge of a cabin roof, and smoke above it. Close to the cabin was a large pole corral. Cheyenne saw the backs of Filaree and Joshua, among the other horses, long before he came to the corral. Yet, not wishing to appear too eager, he said nothing until he arrived at the corner of the fence.

Then he turned and pointed. "Them's my hosses—the gray and the buckskin. I'm mighty glad you caught 'em up."

Sneed nodded. "One of my boys found them in with a bunch of my stock and run them in here."

A few rods from the corral stood the cabin, larger than Cheyenne had imagined, and built of heavy logs, with a wide-roofed porch running across the entire front. On the veranda lay several saddles. Tied to the hitch rail stood two chunky mountain ponies that showed signs of recent hard use.

Cheyenne smiled as he turned toward Sneed. "You got a mighty snug homestead up here, neighbor."

"Tie your horse and step in," invited Sneed.

"He'll stand," said Cheyenne, dismounting and dropping the reins.

Cheyenne was in the enemy's country. But he trusted to his ability to play up to his reputation for an easy-going hobo to get him out again, without trouble. He appeared unaware of the covert suspicion with which Sneed watched his every movement.

"Meet the boys," said Sneed as they entered the cabin.

Cheyenne nodded to the four men who sat playing cards at a long table in the main room. They returned his nod indifferently and went on with their game. Cheyenne pretended an interest in the game, meanwhile studying the visible characteristics of the players. One and all they were hard-boiled, used to the open, rough-spoken, and indifferent to Cheyenne's presence.

Sneed stepped to the kitchen and pulled the coffee-pot to the front of the stove. Finally Cheyenne strolled out to the veranda and seated himself on the long bench near the doorway. He picked up a stick and began to whittle, and as he whittled his gaze traveled from the log stable to the corral, and from there to the edge of the clearing. He heard Sneed speak to one of the men in a low voice. Cheyenne slipped his knife into his pocket and his fingers touched the pair of dice.

He drew out the dice and rattled them. "Go 'way, you snake eyes!" he chanted as he threw the dice along the bench. "Little Jo, where you bushin' out? You sure are bashful!" He threw again. "Roll on, you box-car! I don't like you, nohow! Nine? Nine? Five and a four! Six and a three! Just as easy!"

Sneed came to the doorway and glanced at Cheyenne, who continued shooting craps with himself, oblivious to Sneed's muttered comment. Sneed turned and stepped in. "Crazy as a hoot owl," he said as one of the card-players glanced up.

Cheyenne picked up the dice and listened. He heard Sneed stepping heavily about the kitchen, and he heard an occasional and vivid exclamation from one of the card-players. He glanced at the distant edge of timber. He shook his head. "Can't make it!" he declared, and again he threw the dice.

One of the cubes rolled off the bench. He stooped and picked it up. As he straightened, he stared. Just at the edge of the timber he saw Little Jim's pony, and Little Jim's black hat. Some one in the cabin pushed back a chair. Evidently the card game was finished.

Then Cheyenne heard Sneed's voice: "Just lay off that game, if you want to eat. Come and get it."

Wondering what Little Jim was up to, Cheyenne turned and walked into the cabin. "Guess I'll wash up, first," he said, gazing about as though looking for the wherewithal to wash. He knew well enough where the basin was. He had noticed it out by the kitchen door, when he rode up to the cabin. Sneed told him where to find the basin. Cheyenne stepped round the cabin. Covertly he glanced toward the edge of the timber. Little Jim had disappeared.

Entering the cabin briskly, Cheyenne took his place at the table and ate heartily.

Lawson, who seemed to be Sneed's right-hand man, was the first to speak to him. "Bill tells me you are huntin' hosses."

"Yep! That little gray and the buckskin, out in your corral, are my hosses. They strayed—"

"Didn't see no brand on 'em," declared Lawson.

"Nope. They never was branded. I raised 'em both, when I was workin' for Senator Steve, over to the Box-S."

"That sounds all right. But you got to show me. I bought them cayuses from a Chola, down in the valley."

Cheyenne suspected that Lawson was trying to create argument and, in so doing, open up a way to make him back down and leave or take the consequences of his act in demanding the horses.

"Honest, they're my hosses," declared Cheyenne, turning to Sneed.

"You'll have to talk to Lawson," said Sneed.

Cheyenne frowned and scratched his head. Suddenly his face brightened. "Tell you what I'll do! I'll shoot you craps for 'em."

"That's all right, but what'll you put up against 'em?" asked Lawson.

"What did you pay for 'em?" queried Cheyenne.

"Fifty bucks."

"You got 'em cheap. They're worth that much to me." Cheyenne pushed back his chair and, fishing in his jeans, dug up a purse. "Here's my fifty. As soon as you get through eatin' we'll shoot for the ponies."

Lawson, while finishing his meal, made up his mind that Cheyenne would not get away with that fifty dollars, game or no game; and, also, that he would not get the horses. Cheyenne knew this—knew the kind of man he was dealing with. But he had a reason to keep the men in the cabin. Little Jim was out there somewhere, and up to something. If any of the men happened to catch sight of Little Jim, they would suspect Cheyenne of some trickery. Moreover, if Little Jim were caught—but Cheyenne refused to let himself think of what might happen in that event.

Cheyenne threw the dice on the table as Lawson got up. "Go ahead and shoot."

"Show me what I got to beat," said Lawson.

"All right. Watch 'em close."

Cheyenne gathered up the dice and threw. Calling his point, he snapped his fingers and threw again. The men crowded round, momentarily interested in Cheyenne's sprightly monologue. Happening to glance through the doorway as he gathered up the dice for another throw, Cheyenne noticed that his horse had turned and was standing, with ears and eyes alert, looking toward the corral.

Cheyenne tossed up the dice, caught them and purposely made a wild throw. One of the little cubes shot across the table and clattered on the floor. Cheyenne barely had time to glance through the kitchen doorway and the window beyond as he recovered the cube. But he had seen that the corral bars were down and that the corral was empty. Quickly he resumed his place at the table and threw again, meanwhile talking steadily. He had not made his point nor had he thrown a seven. Sweat prickled on his forehead. Little Jim had seen his father's horses and knew that the men were in the cabin. With the rashness of boyhood he had sneaked up to the corral, dropped the bars, and had then flung pine cones at the horses, starting them to milling and finally to a dash through the gateway and out into the meadow.

Henry Herbert Knibbs

Cheyenne brushed his arm across his face. "Come on you, Filaree!" he chanted.

Somebody would be mightily surprised when the ownership of Filaree and Joshua was finally decided. Unwittingly, Little Jim had placed his father in a still more precarious position. Sneed and his men, finding the corral empty, would naturally conclude that Cheyenne had kept them busy while some friend had run off the horses. Cheyenne knew the risks he ran; but, above all, he wanted to prolong the game until Little Jim got safely beyond reach of Sneed's men. As for himself—

Again Cheyenne threw, but he did not make his point, nor throw a seven. He threw several times; and still he did not make his point. Finally he made his point. Smiling, he gathered up his money and tucked it in his pocket.

"I reckon that settles it," he said cheerfully.

Sneed and Lawson exchanged glances. Cheyenne, rolling a cigarette, drew a chair toward them and sat down. He seemed at home, and altogether friendly. One of the men picked up a deck of cards and suggested a game. Sneed lighted his pipe and stepped to the kitchen to get a drink of water. Cheyenne glanced casually round the cabin, drew his feet under himself, and jumped for the doorway. He heard Sneed drop the dipper and knew that Sneed would pick up something else, and quickly.

Cheyenne made the saddle on the run, reined toward the corral, and, passing it on the run, turned in the saddle to glance back. Sneed was in the doorway. Cheyenne jerked his horse to one side and dug in the spurs. Sneed's rifle barked and a bullet whined past Cheyenne's head. He crouched in the saddle. Again a bullet whistled across the sunlit clearing.

The cow-horse was going strong. A tree flicked past, then another and another.

Cheyenne straightened in the saddle and glanced back through the timber. He saw a jumble of men and horses in front of the cabin. "They got just two hosses handy, and they're rode down," he muttered as he sped through the shadows of the forest.

Across another sun-swept meadow he rode, and into the timber again—and before he realized it he was back on the mountain trail that led to the valley. He took the first long, easy grade on the run, checked at the switchback, and pounded down the succeeding grade, still under cover of the hillside timber, but rapidly nearing the more open country of brush and rock.

As he reined in at the second switchback he saw, far below, and going at a lively trot, seven or eight horses, and behind them, hazing them along as fast as the trail would permit, Little Jim.

"If Sneed's outfit gets to the rim before he makes the next turn, they'll get him sure," reasoned Cheyenne.

He thought of turning back and trying to stop Sneed's men. He thought of turning his horse loose and ambushing the mountainmen, afoot. But Cheyenne did not want to kill. His greatest fear was that Little Jim might get hurt. As he hesitated, a rifle snarled from the rim above, and he saw Little Jim's horse flinch and jump forward.

"I reckon it's up to us, old Steel Dust," he said to his horse.

Hoping to draw the fire of the men above, he eased his horse round the next bend and then spurred him to a run. Below,

Little Jim was jogging along, within a hundred yards or so of the bend that would screen him from sight. Realizing that he could never make the next turn on the run, Cheyenne gripped with his knees, and leaned back to meet the shock as Steel Dust plunged over the end of the turn and crashed through the brush below. A slug whipped through the brush and clipped a twig in front of the horse.

Steel Dust swerved and lunged on down through the heavy brush. A naked creek-bed showed white and shimmering at the bottom of the slope. Again a slug whined through the sunlight and Cheyenne's hat spun from his head and settled squarely on a low bush. It was characteristic of Cheyenne that he grabbed for his hat—and got it as he dashed past.

"Keep the change," said Cheyenne as he ducked beneath a branch and straightened up again. He was almost to the creek-bed, naked to the sunlight, and a bad place to cross with guns going from above. He pulled up, slipped from his horse, and slapped him on the flank.

The pony leaped forward, dashed across the creek-bed, and cut into the trail beyond. A bullet flattened to a silver splash on a boulder. Another bullet shot a spurt of sand into the air. Cheyenne crouched tense, and then made a rush. A slug sang past his head. Heat palpitated in the narrow draw. He gained the opposite bank, dropped, and crawled through the brush and lay panting, close to the trail. From above him somewhere came the note of a bird: *Chirr-up! Chirr-up!* Again a slug tore through the brush scattering twigs and tiny leaves on Cheyenne's hat.

"That one didn't say, 'Cheer up!'" murmured Cheyenne.

When he had caught his breath he crawled out and into the narrow trail. The shooting had ceased. Evidently the men were riding. Stepping round the shoulder of the next bend, he peered up toward the rim of the range. A tiny figure appeared riding down the first long grade, and then another figure. Turning, he saw his own horse quietly nipping at the grass in the crevices of the rocks along the trail.

He walked down to the horse slowly and caught him up. Loosening his carbine from the scabbard, and deeming himself lucky to have it, after that wild ride down the mountain, he stepped back to the angle of the bend, rested the carbine against a rocky shoulder and dropped a shot in front of the first rider, who stopped suddenly and took to cover.

"That'll hold 'em for a spell," said Cheyenne, stepping back. He mounted and rode on down the trail, eyeing the tracks of the horses that Little Jim was hazing toward the valley below. Cheyenne shook his head. "He's done run off the whole dog-gone outfit! There's nothin' stingy about that kid."

Striking to the lower level, Cheyenne cut across country to his camp. He found Bartley leaning comfortably back against a saddle, reading aloud, and opposite him sat Dorry, so intent upon the reading that she did not hear Cheyenne until he spoke.

"Evenin', folks! Seen anything of Jimmy?"

"Oh—Cheyenne! No, have you?" It was Dorothy who spoke, as Bartley closed the book and got to his feet.

"Was you lookin' for Jimmy's address in that there book?" queried Cheyenne, grinning broadly.

Dorothy flushed and glanced at Bartley, who immediately changed the subject by calling attention to Cheyenne's hat.

　　　　　Henry Herbert Knibbs

Cheyenne also changed the subject by stating that Jimmy had recently ridden down the trail toward the ranch—with some horses.

"Then you got your horses?" said Bartley.

"I reckon they're over to the ranch about now."

"Jimmy has been gone all day," said Dorothy. "Aunt Jane is terribly worried about him."

"Jimmy and me took a little ride in the hills," said Cheyenne casually. "But you needn't to tell Aunt Jane that Jimmy was with me. It turned out all right."

"I rode over to your camp to look for Jimmy," said Dorothy, "but Mr. Bartley had not seen him."

Cheyenne nodded and reined his horse round.

"Why, your shirt is almost ripped from your back!" said Bartley.

"My hoss shied, back yonder, and stepped off into the brush. We kept on through the brush. It was shorter."

Dorothy mounted her horse, and, nodding farewell to Bartley, accompanied Cheyenne to the ranch. When they were halfway there, Dorothy, who had been riding thoughtfully along, saying nothing, turned to her companion: "Cheyenne, you had trouble up there. You might at least tell *me* about it."

"Well, Miss Dorry—" And Cheyenne told her how Jimmy had followed him, how he had sent Jimmy back, and the unexpected appearance of that young hopeful in the timber near Sneed's cabin. "I was in there, figurin' hard how to get my hosses and get away, when, somehow, Jimmy got to the corral and turned Sneed's stock loose and hazed 'em down the trail. But where he run 'em to is the joke. I figured he would show up at our camp. It would be just like him to run the whole bunch into the ranch corral. And I reckon he done it."

"But, Mr. Sneed!" exclaimed Dorothy. "If he finds out we had anything to do with running off his horses—"

"He never saw Jimmy clost enough to tell who he was. 'Course, Sneed knows Aunt Jane is my sister, and most he'll suspicion is that I got help from *some* of my folks. But so far he don't know *who* helped me turn the trick."

"You don't seem to be very serious about it," declared Dorothy.

"Serious? Me? Why, ain't most folks serious enough without everybody bein' took that way?"

"Perhaps. But I knew something had happened the minute you rode into camp."

"So did I," asserted Cheyenne, and he spoke sharply to his horse.

Dorothy flushed. "Cheyenne, I rode over to find Jimmy. You needn't—Oh, there's Aunt Jane now! And there's Jimmy, and the corral is full of horses!"

"Reckon we better step along," and Cheyenne put Steel Dust to a lope.

CHAPTER XV

MORE PONY TRACKS

Summoned from the west end of the ranch, where he had been irrigating the alfalfa, Uncle Frank arrived at the house just as Cheyenne and Dorothy rode up. Little Jim was excitedly endeavoring to explain to Aunt Jane how the corral came to be filled with strange horses.

Uncle Frank nodded to Cheyenne and turned to Jimmy. "Where you been?"

"I was over on the mountain."

"How did these horses get here?"

Uncle Frank's eye was stern. Jimmy hesitated. He had been forbidden to go near Sneed's place; and he knew that all that stood between a harness strap and his small jeans was the presence of Dorothy and Cheyenne. It was pretty tough to have recovered the stolen horses single-handed, and then to take a licking for it.

Little Jim gazed hopefully at his father.

"Why, I was chousin' around up there," he explained, "and I

seen dad's hosses, and—and I started 'em down the trail and the whole blame bunch followed 'em. They was travelin' so fast I couldn't cut 'em out, so I just let 'em drift. Filaree and Josh just nacherally headed for the corral and the rest followed 'em in."

Uncle Frank gazed sternly at Jimmy. "Who told you to help your father get his horses?"

"Nobody."

"Did your Aunt Jane tell you you could go over to the mountain?"

"I never asked her."

"You trot right into the house and stay there," said Uncle Frank.

Little Jim cast an appealing glance at Cheyenne and walked slowly toward the house, incidentally and unconsciously rubbing his hand across his jeans with a sort of anticipatory movement. He bit his lip, and the tears started to his eyes. But he shook them away, wondering what he might do to avert the coming storm. Perhaps his father would interpose between him and the dreaded harness strap. Yet Jimmy knew that his father had never interfered when a question of discipline arose.

Suddenly Little Jim's face brightened. He marched through the house to the wash bench, and, unsolicited, washed his hands and face and soaped his hair, after which he slicked it down carefully, so that there might be no mistake about his having brushed and combed it. He rather hoped that Uncle Frank or Aunt Jane would come in just then and find him at this unaccustomed task. It might help.

Meanwhile, Cheyenne and his brother-in-law had a talk, outside. Dorothy and Aunt Jane retired to the veranda, talking in low tones. Presently Little Jim, who could stand the strain no longer,—the jury seemed a long time at arriving at a verdict,—appeared on the front veranda, hatless, washed, and his hair fearfully and wonderfully brushed and combed.

"Why, Jimmy!" exclaimed Dorothy.

Jimmy fidgeted and glanced away bashfully. Presently he stole to his Aunt Jane's side.

"Am I goin' to get a lickin'?" he queried.

Aunt Jane shook her head, and patted his hand. Entrenched beside Aunt Jane, Jimmy watched his father and Uncle Frank as they talked by the big corral. Uncle Frank was gesturing toward the mountains. Cheyenne was arguing quietly.

"It ain't just the runnin' off of Sneed's hosses," said Uncle Frank. "That's bad enough. But I told Jimmy to keep away from Sneed's."

"So did I," declared Cheyenne. "And seein' as I'm his dad, it's up to me to lick him if he's goin' to get licked."

"Sneed is like to ride down some night and set fire to the barns," asserted Uncle Frank.

"Sneed don't know yet who run off his stock. And he can't say that I did, and prove it. Now, Frank, you just hold your hosses. I'll ride over to camp and get my outfit together and come over here. Then we'll throw Steve Brown's hosses into your pasture, and I'll see that Sneed's stock is out of here, pronto."

"That's all right. But Sneed will trail his stock down here."

"But he won't find 'em here. And he'll never know they was in your corral."

Uncle Frank shook his head doubtfully. He was a pessimist and always argued the worst of a possible situation.

"And before I'll see Jimmy take a lickin'—this trip—I'll ride back and shoot it out with Sneed and his outfit," stated Cheyenne.

"I reckon you're fool enough to do it," said Uncle Frank.

* * * * *

An hour later Bartley and Cheyenne were at the Lawrence ranch, where they changed packs, saddled Filaree and Joshua, and turned the horses borrowed from Steve Brown into Uncle Frank's back pasture.

Little Jim watched these operations with keen interest. He wanted to help, but refrained for fear that he would muss up his hair—and he wanted Uncle Frank to notice his hair as it was.

Aunt Jane hastily prepared a meal and Dorothy helped.

In a few minutes Cheyenne and Bartley had eaten, and were ready for the road. Cheyenne stepped up and shook hands with Jimmy, as though Jimmy were a grown-up. Jimmy felt elated. There was no one just like his father, even if folks did say that Cheyenne Hastings could do better than ride around the country singing and joking with everybody.

"And don't forget to stop by when you come back," said

Aunt Jane, bidding farewell to Bartley.

Dorothy shook hands with the Easterner and wished him a pleasant journey, rather coolly, Bartley thought. She was much more animated when bidding farewell to Cheyenne.

"And I won't forget to send you that rifle," said Bartley as he nodded to Little Jim.

Uncle Frank helped them haze Sneed's horses out of the yard on to the road, where Cheyenne waited to head them from taking the hill trail, again.

Just as he left, Bartley turned to Dorothy who stood twisting a pomegranate bud in her fingers. "May I have it?" he asked, half in jest.

She tossed the bud to him and he caught it. Then he spurred out after Cheyenne who was already hazing the horses down the road. Occasionally one of the horses tried to break out and take to the hills, but Cheyenne always headed it back to the bunch, determined, for some reason unknown to Bartley, to keep the horses together and going south.

The road climbed gradually, winding in and out among the foothills. As the going became stiffer, the rock outcropped and the dust settled.

The horses slowed to a walk. Bartley wondered why his companion seemed determined to drive Sneed's stock south. He thought it would be just as well to let them break for the hills, and not bother with them. But Cheyenne offered no explanation. He evidently knew what he was about.

To their right lay the San Andreas Valley across which the long, slanting shadows of sunset crept slowly. Still Cheyenne kept the bunch of horses going briskly, when the going permitted speed. Just over a rise they came suddenly upon an Apache, riding a lean, active paint horse. Cheyenne pulled up and talked with the Indian. The latter grinned, nodded, and, jerking his pony round, rode after the horses as they drifted ahead. Bartley saw the Apache bunch the animals again, and turn them off the road toward the hills.

"Didn't expect to meet up with luck, so soon," declared Cheyenne. "I figured to turn Sneed's hosses loose when I'd got 'em far enough from the ranch. But that Injun'll take care of 'em. Sneed ain't popular with the Apaches. Sneed's cabin is right clost to the res'avation line."

"What will the Indian do with the horses?" queried Bartley.

"Most like trade 'em to his friends."

Bartley gestured toward a spot of green far across the valley. "Looks like a town," he said.

"San Andreas—and that's where we stop, to-night. No campin' in the brush for me while Sneed is ridin' the country lookin' for his stock. It wouldn't be healthy."

CHAPTER XVI

SAN ANDREAS TOWN

A sleepy town, that paid little attention to the arrival or departure of strangers, San Andreas in the valley merely rubbed its eyes and dozed again as Cheyenne and Bartley rode in, put up their horses at the livery, and strolled over to the adobe hotel where they engaged rooms for the night.

Bartley was taken by the picturesque simplicity of the place, and next morning he suggested that they stay a few days and enjoy the advantage of having some one other than themselves cook their meals and make their beds. The hotel, a relic of old times, with its patio and long portal, its rooms whose lower floors were on the ground level, its unpretentious spaciousness, appealed strongly to Bartley as something unusual in the way of a hostelry. It seemed restful, romantic, inviting. It was a place where a man might write, dream, loaf, and smoke. Then, incidentally, it was not far from the Lawrence ranch, which was not far from the home of a certain young woman whom Little Jim called "Dorry."

Bartley thought that Dorothy was rather nice—in fact, singularly interesting. He had not imagined that a Western girl could be so thoroughly domestic, natural, charming, and at the same time manage a horse so well. He had visioned

Western girls as hard-voiced horse-women, masculine, bold, and rather scornful of a man who did not wear chaps and ride broncos. True, Dorothy was not like the girls in the East. She seemed less sophisticated—less inclined to talk small talk just for its own sake; yet, concluded Bartley, she was utterly feminine and quite worth while.

Cheyenne smiled as Bartley suggested that they stay in San Andreas a few days; and Cheyenne nodded in the direction from which they had come.

"I kinda like this part of the country, myself," he said, "but I hate to spend all my money in one place."

Bartley suddenly realized that his companion, was nothing more than a riding hobo, a vagrant, without definite means of support, and disinclined to stay in any one place long.

"I'll take care of the expenses," said Bartley.

Cheyenne smiled, but shook his head. "It ain't that, right now. Me, I got to shoot that there game of craps with Panhandle, and I figure he won't ride this way."

"But you have recovered your horses," argued Bartley.

Cheyenne gestured toward the south. "I reckon I'll keep movin', pardner. And that game of craps is as good a excuse as I want."

"I had hoped that it would be plain sailing, from now on," declared Bartley. "I thought of stopping here only three or four days. This sort of town is new to me."

"They's lots like it, between here and the border," said Cheyenne. "But I don't want no 'dobe walls between me and the sky-line, reg'lar. I can stand it for a day, mebby."

"Well, perhaps we may agree to dissolve partnership temporarily," suggested Bartley. "I think I'll stay here a few days, at least."

"That's all right, pardner. I don't aim to tell no man how to live. But me, I aim to live in the open."

"Do you think that man Sneed will ride down this way?" queried Bartley, struck by a sudden idea.

"That ain't why I figure to keep movin'," said Cheyenne. "But seein' as you figure to stay, I'll stick around to-day, and light out to-morrow mornin'. Mebby you'll change your mind, and come along."

Bartley spent the forenoon with Cheyenne, prowling about the old town, interested in its quaint unusualness. The afternoon heat drove him to the shade of the hotel veranda, and, feeling unaccountably drowsy, he finally went to his room, and, stretching out on the bed, fell asleep. He was awakened by Cheyenne's knock at the door. Supper was ready.

After supper they strolled out to the street and watched the town wake up. From down the street a ways came the sound of a guitar and singing. A dog began to howl. Then came a startled yelp, and the howl died away in the dusk. The singing continued. A young Mexican in a blue serge suit, tan shoes, and with a black sombrero set aslant on his head, walked down the street beside a Mexican girl, young, fat, and giggling. They passed the hotel with all the self-consciousness of being attired in their holiday raiment.

A wagon rattled past and stopped at the saloon a few doors

down the street. Then a ragged Mexican, hazing two tired burros, appeared in the dim light cast from a window—a quaint silhouette that merged in the farther shadows. Cheyenne moved his feet restlessly.

Bartley smiled. "The road for mine," he quoted.

Cheyenne nodded. "Reckon I'll go see how the hosses are makin' it."

"I'll walk over with you," said Bartley.

As they came out of the livery barn again, Bartley happened to glance at the lighted doorway of the cantina opposite. From within the saloon came the sound of glasses clinking occasionally, and voices engaged in lazy conversation. Cheyenne fingered the dice in his pocket and hummed a tune. Slowly he moved toward the lighted doorway, and Bartley walked beside him.

"I got a thirst," stated Cheyenne.

Bartley laughed. "Well, as we are about to dissolve partnership, I don't mind taking one myself."

"Tough joint," declared Cheyenne as he stepped up to the doorway.

"All the better," said Bartley.

A young rancher, whose team stood at the hitch-rail, nodded pleasantly as they entered.

"Mescal," said Cheyenne, and he laid a silver dollar on the bar.

Henry Herbert Knibbs

Bartley glanced about the low-ceilinged room. The place, poorly lighted with oil lamps, looked sinister enough to satisfy the most hardy adventurer, although it was supposed to be a sort of social center for the enjoyment of vino and talk. The bar was narrow, made of some kind of soft wood, and painted blue. The top of it was almost paintless in patches.

Back of the bar a narrow shelf, also painted blue, offered a lean choice of liquors. Several Mexicans lounged at the side tables along the wall. The young American rancher stood at the bar, drinking. The proprietor, a fat, one-eyed Mexican whose face was deeply pitted from smallpox, served Bartley and Cheyenne grudgingly. The mescal was fiery stuff. Bartley coughed as he swallowed it.

"Why not just whiskey, and have it over with?" he queried, grinning at Cheyenne.

"Whiskey ain't whiskey, here," Cheyenne replied. "But mescal is just what she says she is. I like to know the kind of poison I'm drinkin'."

Bartley began to experience an inner glow that was not unpleasant. Once down, this native Mexican drink was not so bad. He laid a coin on the bar and the glasses were filled again.

Cheyenne nodded and drank Bartley's health. Bartley suggested that they sit at one of the side tables and study the effects of mescal on the natives present.

"Let joy be unconfined," said Cheyenne.

"Where in the world did you get that?"

"Oh, I can read," declared Cheyenne. "Before I took to ramblin', I used to read some, nights. I reckon that's where I got the idea of makin' up po'try, later."

"I really beg your pardon," said Bartley.

"The mescal must of told you."

"I don't quite get that," said Bartley.

"No? Well, you ain't the first. Josh and Filaree is the only ones that sabes me. Let's sit in this corner and watch the mescal work for a livin'."

It was a hot night. Sweat prickled on Bartley's forehead. His nose itched. He lit a cigar. It tasted bitter, so he asked Cheyenne for tobacco and papers, and rolled a cigarette. He inhaled a whiff, and felt more comfortable. The Mexicans, who had ceased to talk when Bartley and Cheyenne entered, were now at it again, making plenty of noise.

Cheyenne hummed to himself and tapped the floor with his boot-heel. "She's a funny old world," he declared.

Bartley nodded and blew a smoke-ring.

"Miss Dorry's sure a interestin' girl," asserted Cheyenne.

Bartley nodded again.

"Kind of young and innocent-like."

Again Bartley nodded.

"It ain't a bad country to settle down in, for folks that likes to settle," said Cheyenne.

Bartley glanced sharply at his companion. Cheyenne was gazing straight ahead. His face was unreadable.

"Now if I was the settlin' kind—" He paused and slowly turned toward Bartley. "A man could raise alfalfa and chickens and kids."

"Go ahead," laughed Bartley.

"I'm goin'—to-morrow mornin'. And you say you figure to stay here a spell?"

"Oh, just a few days. I imagine I shall grow tired of it. But to-night, I feel pretty well satisfied to stay right where I am."

Cheyenne rose and strode to the bar. After a short argument with the proprietor, he returned with a bottle and glasses. Bartley raised his eyebrows questioningly.

"Once in a while—" And Cheyenne gestured toward the bottle.

"It's powerful stuff," said Bartley.

"We ain't far from the hotel," declared Cheyenne. And he filled their glasses.

"This ought to be the last, for me," said Bartley, drinking. "But don't let that make any difference to you."

Cheyenne drank and shrugged his shoulders. He leaned back and gazed at the opposite wall. Bartley vaguely realized that the Mexicans were chattering, that two or three persons had come in, and that the atmosphere was heavy with tobacco smoke. He unbuttoned his shirt-collar.

Presently Cheyenne twisted round in his chair. "Remember Little Jim, back at the Hastings ranch?"

"I should say so! It would be difficult to forget him."

"Miss Dorry thinks a heap of that kid."

"She seems to."

"Now, I ain't drunk," Cheyenne declared solemnly. "I sure wish I was. You know Little Jim is my boy. Well, his ma is livin' over to Laramie. She writ to me to come back to her, onct. I reckon Sears got tired of her. She lived with him a spell after she quit me. Folks say Sears treated her like a dog. I guess I wasn't man enough, when I heard that—"

"You mean Panhandle Sears—at Antelope?"

"Him."

"Oh, I see!" said Bartley slowly. "And that crap game, at Antelope—I see!"

"If Panhandle had a-jumped me, instead of you, that night, I'd 'a' killed him. Do you know why Wishful stepped in and put Sears down? Wishful did that so that there wouldn't be a killin'. That's the second time Sears has had his chance to git me, but he won't take that chance. That's the second time we met up since—since my wife left me. The third time it'll be lights out for somebody. I ain't drunk."

"Then Sears has got a yellow streak?"

"Any man that uses a woman rough has. When Jimmy's ma left us, I reckon I went loco. It wa'n't just her *leavin'* us. But when I heard she had took up with Sears, and knowin' what

Henry Herbert Knibbs

he was—I just quit. I was workin' down here at the ranch, then. I went up North, figurin' to kill him. Folks thought I was yellow, for not killin' him. They think so right now. Mebby I am.

"I worked up North a spell, but I couldn't stay. So I lit out and come down South again. First time I met up with Sears was over on the Tonto. He stepped up and slapped my face, in front of a crowd, in the Lone Star. And I took it. But I told him I'd sure see him again, and give him another chance to slap my face.

"You see, Panhandle Sears is that kind—he's got to work himself up to kill a man. And over there at Antelope, that night, he just about knowed that if he lifted a finger, I'd git him. He figured to start a ruckus, and then git me in the mix-up. Wishful was on, and he stopped that chance. Folks think that because I come ridin' and singin' and joshin' that I ain't no account. Mebby I ain't."

Cheyenne poured another drink for himself. Bartley declined to drink again. He was thinking of this squalid tragedy and of its possible outcome. The erstwhile sprightly Cheyenne held a new significance for the Easterner. That a man could ride up and down the trails singing, and yet carry beneath it all the grim intent some day to kill a man—

Bartley felt that Cheyenne had suddenly become a stranger, an unknown quantity, a sinister jester, in fact, a dangerous man. He leaned forward and touched Cheyenne's arm.

"Why not give up the idea of—er—getting Sears; and settle down, and make a home for Little Jim?"

"When Aunt Jane took him, the understandin' was that Jimmy was to be raised respectable, which is the same as tellin' me that I don't have nothin' to do with raisin' him. Me, I got to keep movin'."

Bartley turned toward the doorway as a tall figure loomed through the haze of tobacco smoke: a gaunt, heavy-boned man, bearded and limping slightly. With him were several companions, booted and spurred; evidently just in from a hard ride.

Cheyenne turned to Bartley. "That's Bill Sneed—and his crowd. I ain't popular with 'em—right now."

CHAPTER XVII

THAT MESCAL

"The man who had your horses?" queried Bartley.

Cheyenne nodded. "The one at the end of the bar. The hombre next to him is Lawson, who claims he bought my hosses from a Mexican, down here. Lawson is the one that is huntin' trouble. Sneed don't care nothin' about a couple of cayuses. He won't start anything. He's here just to back up Lawson if things git interestin'."

"But what can they do? We're here, in town, minding our own business. They know well enough that Panhandle stole your horses. And you said the people in San Andreas don't like Sneed a whole lot."

"Because they're scared of him and his crowd. And we're strangers here. It's just me and Lawson, this deal. Sneed is sizin' you up, back of his whiskers, right now. He's tryin' to figure out who you are. Sneed ain't one to run into the law when they's anybody lookin' on. He works different.

"Now, while he is figurin', you just git up easy and step out and slip over to the barn and saddle up Joshua. I'm goin' to need him. Take the tie-rope off Filaree and leave him loose in his stall. Just say 'Adios' to me when you git up, like you was goin' back to the hotel. And if you'll settle what we owe—"

"That's all right. But my feet aren't cold, yet."

"You figure to stay in town a spell, don't you? Well, I figure to leave, right soon. I'm tryin' to dodge trouble. It's your chanct to help out."

"Why can't we both walk out?"

"'Cause they'd follow us. They won't follow you."

Bartley glanced at the men ranged along the bar, rose, and, shaking hands with Cheyenne, strode out, nodding pleasantly to the one-eyed proprietor as he went.

Sneed eyed the Easterner sharply, and nudged one of his men as Bartley passed through the doorway.

"Just step out and see where he goes, Hull," he ordered in an undertone. "Keep him in sight."

The man spoken to hitched up his chaps, and, turning to finish his drink, strolled out casually.

Bartley saw a row of saddle-horses tied at the rail. He noticed the slickers on the saddles and the carbines under the stirrup leathers. It was evident that the riders were not entirely on pleasure bent. He crossed the street, wakened the stableman, paid the bill, and saddled Joshua. Then he took the tie-rope off Filaree, as Cheyenne had directed. Bartley led Joshua through the barn to the back, where he was tying him to a wagon wheel when a figure loomed up in the semi-darkness.

"Ridin', stranger?"

The figure struck a match and lighted a cigarette. Bartley at once recognized him as one of Sneed's men. Resenting the other's question and his attitude of easy familiarity, Bartley ignored his presence.

"Hard of hearin'?" queried Hull.

"Rather."

"I said: Was you ridin'?"

"Yesterday," replied Bartley.

Hull blew a whiff of smoke in Bartley's face. It seemed casual, but was intended as an insult. Bartley flushed, and realizing that the other was there to intercept any action on his part to aid Cheyenne, he dropped Joshua's reins, and without the slightest warning of his intent—in fact, Hull thought the Easterner was stooping to pick up the reins—Bartley launched a haymaker that landed with a loud crack on Hull's unguarded chin, and Hull's head snapped back. Bartley jumped forward and shot another one to the same spot. Hull's head hit the edge of the doorway as he went down.

He lay there, inert, a queer blur in the half-light. Bartley licked his skinned knuckles.

"He may resent this, when he wakes up," he murmured. "I believe I'll tie him."

Bartley took Joshua's tie-rope and bound Mr. Hull's arms and legs, amateurishly, but securely.

Then he strode through to the front of the barn. He could hear loud talking in the saloon opposite and thought he could distinguish Cheyenne's voice. Bartley wondered what would happen in there, and when things would begin to pop, if there was to be any popping. He felt foolishly helpless and inefficient—rather a poor excuse for a partner, just then. Yet there was that husky rider, back there in the straw. He was even more helpless and inefficient. Bartley licked his knuckles, and grinned.

"There must have been a little mescal in that second punch," he thought. "I never hit so hard in my life."

The stableman had retired to his bunk—a habit of night stablemen. The stable was dark and still, save for the munching of the horses. In the saloon across the way Cheyenne was facing Sneed and his men, alone. Bartley felt like a quitter. Indecision irritated him, and curiosity urged him to do something other than to stand staring at the saloon front. He recalled his plan to sojourn in San Andreas a few days, and incidently to ride over to the Lawrence ranch— frankly, to have another visit with Dorothy. He shrugged his shoulders. That idea now seemed insignificant, compared with the present possibilities.

"I'm a free agent," he soliloquized. "I think I'll take a hand in this, myself."

He snapped his fingers as he turned and hastened to Dobe's stall. He led Dobe out to the stable floor, got his saddle from the office, told the sleepy stableman that he was going to take a little ride, and saddled Dobe. And he led Dobe back to where Joshua was tied. He had forgotten his victim on the floor, for a moment, but was aware of him when he stumbled over him in the dark. The other mumbled and struggled faintly.

"I left your gun in the wagon-box," said Bartley. "I wouldn't move around much, if I were you. One of the horses might step on your face and hurt his foot."

Mr. Hull was not pleased at this, and he said as much. Bartley tied Dobe to the back of the wagon.

"Just keep your eye on the horses a minute," he told Hull. "I'll be back soon."

Bartley felt unusually and inexplicably elated. He had not realized the extreme potency of mescal. The proprietor of the hotel was mildly surprised when Bartley, remarking that he had been called away unexpectedly, paid the hotel bill. Bartley hastened back to the stable. Across the way the horses of the mountain men drowsed in the faint lamplight. Turning, Bartley saw Joshua and Dobe dimly silhouetted in the opening at the far end of the stable. Cheyenne was still in the saloon.

Bartley grinned. "It might help," he said as he stepped across the street. Taking down the rope from the nearest horse, he tied the end of the rope in the horse's bridle and threaded the end through the bridles of all five horses, tying the loose end to the last horse's bridle. "Just like stringing fish!" he murmured soulfully. "When those gentlemen from the interior try to mount, there'll be something doing."

He had just turned to walk back to the stable when he heard a shot, and the lighted doorway of the saloon became suddenly dark. Without waiting to see what would happen next, Bartley ran to the rear of the stable and untied the horses. Behind him he heard the quick trample of feet. He turned. A figure appeared in the front doorway of the stable, a figure that dashed toward him, and, with a leap and a swing, mounted Joshua and spurred out and down the alley back of the building.

Bartley grabbed for his own stirrup, missed it, grabbed again and swung up. Dobe leaped after the other horse, turned at the end of the alley, and, reaching into a long, swinging gallop, pounded across the night-black open. San Andreas had but one street. The backs of its buildings opened to space.

Ahead, Cheyenne thundered across a narrow bridge over an arroyo. Dobe lifted and leaped forward, as though in a race. From behind came the quick patter of hoofs. One of Sneed's men had evidently managed to get his horse loose from the reata. A solitary house, far out on the level, flickered past. Bartley glanced back. The house door opened. A ray of yellow light shot across the road.

"Hey, Cheyenne!" called Bartley.

But Cheyenne's little buckskin was drumming down the night road at a pace that astonished the Easterner. Dobe seemed to be doing his best, yet he could not overtake the buckskin. Behind Bartley the patter of hoofs sounded nearer. Bartley thought he heard Cheyenne call back to him. He leaned forward, but the drumming of hoofs deadened all other sound.

They were on a road, now—a road that ran south across the spaces, unwinding itself like a tape flung from a reel. Suddenly Cheyenne pulled to a stop. Bartley raced up, bracing himself as the big cow-horse set up in two jumps.

"I thought you was abidin' in San Andreas," said Cheyenne.

"There's some one coming!" warned Bartley, breathing heavily.

"And his name is Filaree," declared Cheyenne. "You sure done a good job. Let's keep movin'." And Cheyenne let Joshua out as Filaree drew alongside and nickered shrilly.

"Now I reckon we better hold 'em in a little," said Cheyenne after they had gone, perhaps, a half-mile. "We got a good start."

They slowed the horses to a trot. Filaree kept close to Joshua's flank. A gust of warm air struck their faces.

"Ain't got time to shake hands, pardner," said Cheyenne. "Know where you're goin'?"

"South," said Bartley.

"Correc'. And I don't hear no hosses behind us."

"I strung them together on a rope," said Bartley.

"How's that?"

"I tied Sneed's horses together, with a rope. Ran it through the bridles—like stringing fish. Not according to Hoyle, but it seems to have worked."

Cheyenne shook his head. He did not quite get the significance of Bartley's statement.

"Any one get hurt?" queried Bartley presently.

"Nope. I spoiled a lamp, and I reckon I hit somebody on the head, in the dark, comin' through. Seems like I stepped on somethin' soft, out there back of the barn. It grunted like a human. But I didn't stop to look."

"I had to do it," declared Bartley ambiguously.

"Had to do what?"

"Punch a fellow that wanted to know what I was doing with your horse. I let him have it twice."

"Then you didn't hit him with your gun?"

"No. I wish I had. I've got a fist like a boiled ham. I can feel it swell, right now."

"That there mescal is sure pow'ful stuff."

"Thanks!" said Bartley succinctly.

"Got a kick like white lightin'," said Cheyenne.

"And I paid our hotel bill," continued Bartley.

"Well, that was mighty thoughtful. I plumb forgot it."

Henry Herbert Knibbs

CHAPTER XVIII

JOE SCOTT

Just before daybreak Cheyenne turned from the road and picked his way through the scattered brush to a gulch in the western foothills. Cheyenne's horses seemed to know the place, when they stopped at a narrow, pole gate across the upper end of the gulch, for on beyond the gate the horses again stopped of their own accord. Bartley could barely discern the outlines of a cabin. Cheyenne hallooed.

A muffled answer from the cabin, then a twinkle of light, then the open doorway framing a gigantic figure.

"That you, Shy?" queried the figure.

"Me and a friend."

"You're kind of early," rumbled the figure as the riders dismounted.

"Shucks! You'd be gettin' up, anyway, right soon. We come early so as not to delay your breakfast."

In the cabin, Cheyenne and the big man shook hands. Bartley was introduced. The man was a miner, named Joe Scott.

"Joe, here, is a minin' man—when he ain't runnin' a all-night lunch-stand," explained Cheyenne. "He can't work his placer when it's dark, but he sure can work a skillet and a coffee-mill."

"What you been up to?" queried the giant slowly, as he made a fire in the stove, and set about getting breakfast.

"Up to Clubfoot Sneed's place, to get a couple of hosses that belonged to me. He was kind of hostile. Followed us down to San Andreas and done spoiled our night's rest. But I got the hosses."

"Hosses seems to be his failin'," said the big man.

"So some folks say. I'm one of 'em."

"How are the folks up Antelope way?"

"Kinda permanent, as usual. I hear Panhandle's drifted south again. Wishful, he shoots craps, reg'lar."

Scott nodded, shifted the coffee-pot and sat down on the edge of his bunk. "Got any smokin'?" he queried presently.

Bartley offered the miner a cigar. "I'm afraid it's broken," apologized Bartley.

"That's all right. I was goin' to town this mornin', to get some tobacco and grub. But this will help." And doubling the cigar Scott thrust it in his mouth and chewed it with evident satisfaction.

The gray edge of dawn crept into the room. Scott blew out the light and opened the door.

Bartley felt suddenly sleepy and he drowsed and nodded, realizing that Scott and Cheyenne were talking, and that the faint aroma of coffee drifted toward him, mingling with the chill, fresh air of morning. He pulled himself together and drank the coffee and ate some bacon. From time to time he glanced at Scott, fascinated by the miner's tremendous forearms, his mighty chest and shoulders. Even Cheyenne, who was a fair-sized man, appeared like a boy beside the miner. Bartley wondered that such tremendous strength should be isolated, hidden back there behind the foothills. Yet Scott himself, easy-going and dryly humorous, was evidently content right where he was.

Later the miner showed Bartley about the diggings, quietly proud of his establishment, and enthusiastic about the unfailing supply of water—in fact, Scott talked more about water than he did about gold. Bartley realized that the big miner would have been a misfit in town, that he belonged in the rugged hills from which he wrested a scant six dollars a day by herculean toil.

In a past age, Scott would have been a master builder of castles or of triremes or a maker of armor, but never a fighting man. It was evident that the miner was, despite his great strength, a man of peace. Bartley rather regretted, for some romantic reason or other, that the big miner was not a fighting man.

Yet when they returned to the shack, where Cheyenne sat smoking, Bartley learned that Big Joe Scott had a reputation in his own country. That was when Scott suggested that they needed sleep. He spread a blanket-roll on the cabin floor for Cheyenne and offered Bartley his bunk. Then Scott picked up his rifle and strode across to a shed. Cheyenne pulled off his boots, stretched out on the blanket-roll, and sighed comfortably. Bartley could see the big miner busily twisting something in his hands, something that looked like a leather bag from which occasional tiny spurts of silver gleamed and trickled. Bartley wondered what Scott was doing. He asked Cheyenne.

"He's squeezin' 'quick.'" And Cheyenne explained the process of squeezing quicksilver through a chamois skin. "And I'm glad it ain't my neck," added Cheyenne. "Joe killed a man, with his bare hands, onct. That's why he never gets in a fight, nowadays. He dassn't. 'Course, he had to kill that man, or get killed."

"I noticed he picked up his rifle," said Bartley.

"Nobody'll disturb our sleep," said Cheyenne drowsily.

* * * * *

The afternoon shadows were long when Bartley awakened. Through the doorway he could see Cheyenne out in the shed, talking with Joe Scott.

"Hello!" called Bartley, sitting up. "Lost any horses, Cheyenne?"

Presently Scott and Cheyenne came over to the cabin.

"I'm cook, this trip," stated Cheyenne as he bustled about the kitchen. "I reckon Joe needs a rest. He ain't lookin' right strong."

An early supper, and the three men forgathered outside the cabin and smoked and talked until long after dark. Cheyenne had told Scott of the happenings since leaving Antelope, and jokingly he referred to San Andreas and Bartley's original plan of staying there awhile.

Bartley nodded. "And now that the smoke has blown away, I think I'll go back and finish my visit," he said.

Cheyenne's face expressed surprise and disappointment. "Honest?" he queried.

"Why not?" asked Bartley, and it was a hard question to answer.

After all, Bartley had stuck to him when trouble seemed inevitable, reasoned Cheyenne.

Now the Easterner felt free to do as he pleased. And why shouldn't he? There had been no definite or even tentative agreement as to when they would dissolve partnership. And Bartley's evident determination to carry out his original plan struck Cheyenne as indicative of considerable spirit. It was plain that Sneed's unexpected presence in San Andreas had not affected Bartley very much. With a tinge of malice, born of disappointment, Cheyenne suggested to Bartley that the man he had knocked out, back of the livery barn, would no doubt be glad to see him again.

Bartley turned to Joe Scott. "He's trying to 'Out-West' me a bit, isn't he?"

Scott laughed heartily. "Cheyenne is getting tired of rambling up and down the country alone. He wants a pardner. Seems he likes your company, from what he says. But you can't take him serious. He'll be singin' that everlastin' trail song of his next."

"He hasn't sung much, recently."

Cheyenne bridled and snorted like a colt. "Huh! Just try this on your piano." And seemingly improvising, he waved his arm toward the burro corral.

> One time I had a right good pal,
> Git along, cayuse, git along;
> But he quit me cold for a little ranch gal,
> Git along, cayuse, git along.
>
> And now he's took to pitchin' hay
> On a rancho down San Andreas way;
> He's done tied up and he's got to stay;
> Git along, cayuse, git along.

"I was just learnin' him the ropes, and he quit me cold," complained Cheyenne, appealing to Scott.

"He aims to keep out of trouble," suggested Scott.

"I ain't got no friends," said Cheyenne, grinning.

"Thanks for that," said Scott.

Cheyenne reached in his pocket and drew out the dice. His eyes brightened. He rattled the dice and shot them across the hardpacked ground near the doorstep. Then he struck a match to see what he had thrown. "I'm hittin' the road five minutes after six, to-morrow mornin'," he declared, as he picked up the dice.

CHAPTER XIX

DORRY COMES TO TOWN

At six, next morning, Bartley and Scott were on their way to San Andreas, Bartley riding Dobe and Scott hazing two pack-burros. They took a hill trail, which, Scott explained, was shorter by miles than the valley road which Cheyenne and Bartley had taken to the gulch. Cheyenne was forced to stay at the miner's cabin until Scott returned with the pack-saddle and outfit left in the livery. Scott was after supplies and tobacco.

At first Cheyenne had thought of going along with them. But he reconsidered. He did not care to risk being arrested in San Andreas for having disturbed the peace. If the authorities should happen to detain him, there would be one broken head, one broken lamp, and possibly five or six witnesses as evidence that he had been the aggressor in the saloon. Sneed and his men would swear to anything, and the owner of the saloon would add his bit of evidence. Bartley himself was liable to arrest for assault and battery should Hull lodge a complaint against him. Incidentally, Hull had been found by the stableman, curiously roped and tied and his lower jaw somewhat out of plumb.

Bartley and Scott arrived in San Andreas about noon, saw to their stock and had dinner together. Bartley engaged a room at the hotel. Scott bought supplies. Then, unknown to Bartley, Scott hunted up the town marshal and told him that the Easterner was a friend of his. The town marshal took the hint. Scott assured the marshal that, if Sneed or his men made any trouble in San Andreas, he would gladly come over and help the marshal establish peace. Cheyenne's name was not mentioned.

An hour later Scott appeared in front of the hotel with his burros packed. Bartley, loafing on the veranda, rose and stepped out.

"If you got time," said Scott, "you might walk along with me, out to the edge of town."

Bartley wondered what Scott had in mind, but he agreed to the suggestion at once.

Together they trudged through the sleepy town until they reached the open.

"I guess you can find your way back," said Scott, his eyes twinkling. "And, say, it's a good idea not to pack a shootin'-iron—and let folks know you don't pack one."

"I think I understand," said Bartley.

"Ride over to my camp, any time, and if I'm not there, just make yourself to home." And the big miner turned and started his burros toward the hills.

"Give my regards to Cheyenne," called Bartley.

The miner nodded.

Henry Herbert Knibbs

On his way back through town, Bartley wondered why the miner had asked him to take that walk. Then suddenly he thought of a reason. They had been seen in San Andreas, walking and talking together. That would intimate that they were friends. And a man would have to be blind, not to realize that it would be a mistake to pick a quarrel with Scott, or one of his friends. Joe Scott never quarreled; but he had the reputation of being a man of whom it was safe to step around.

With his sleeves rolled up, sitting in the quiet of his room, Bartley spent the afternoon jotting down notes for a story. He thought he had experienced enough adventure to make a good beginning. Of course, the love element was lacking, yet he thought that might be supplied, later. He had a heroine in mind. Bartley laid down his pencil, and sat back, shaping daydreams. It was hot in the room. It would be cooler down on the veranda. Well, he would finish his rough sketch of Cheyenne, and then step down to the veranda. He caught himself drowsing over his work. He sat up, scribbled a while, nodded sleepily, and, finally, with his head on his arms, he fell asleep.

The rattle of wagon wheels wakened him. A ranch team had just pulled up to the hitch-rail in front of the hotel and a small boy was tying the horses. The boy's hat seemed familiar to Bartley. Then Bartley heard a voice. Suddenly he was wide awake. Little Jim was down there, talking to some one. Bartley rose and peered down. Little Jim's companion was Dorothy. Bartley could not see her face, because of her wide hat-brim. Stepping back into the room, Bartley picked up his pencil and, leaning out of the window, started it rolling down the gentle slope of the veranda roof. It dropped at Dorothy's feet. She started and glanced up. Bartley waved a greeting and disappeared from the window.

Decently clothed, and, imagining that he was in his right mind, he hastened downstairs.

Little Jim expressed no surprise at seeing Bartley, but the youngster's eyes were eager.

He shook hands, like a grown-up. "Got that twenty-two, yet?"

"Haven't seen one, Jimmy. But I won't forget."

"There's a brand-new twenty-two over to Hodges' store, in the window," declared Little Jim.

"That so? Then we'll have to walk over and look at it."

"I done *looked* at it already," said Little Jim.

"Well, then, let's go and price it."

"I done priced it. It's twelve-fifty."

"Well, what do you say to going over and buying it?"

"Sure! Is dad gone?"

"Yes. He left here last night. I thought Miss Gray was with you," said Bartley.

"Sure! She had to come to town to buy some things. She's over to Hodges' now."

Dorothy had not waited for him to appear. Bartley was a bit piqued. But he asked himself why should he be? They were the merest acquaintances. True, they had spent several hours together, reading and discussing verse. But no doubt that had been purely impersonal, on her part. With Little Jim as his guide, Bartley entered Hodges' general store. Dorothy was at the back of the store making purchases. Bartley watched her a moment. He felt a tug at his sleeve.

"The guns is over on this side," declared Little Jim.

"We'll have to wait until Mr. Hodges gets through waiting on Miss Gray," said Bartley.

Little Jim scampered across the aisle and stood on tiptoe peering into a showcase. There were pistols, cheap watches, and a pair of spurs.

Little Jim gazed a moment and then shot over to Dorothy. "Say, Dorry, can't you hurry up? Me and Mr. Bartley are waitin' to look at that twenty-two in the window."

"Now, Jimmy! Oh, how do you do!" And Dorothy greeted Bartley with considerable poise for a young woman who was as interested in the Easterner as she was.

"Don't let us interrupt you," said Bartley. "Our business can wait."

Little Jim scowled, and grimaced at Dorothy, who excused herself to Bartley and went on making her purchases. They were really insignificant purchases—some pins, some thread, and a roll of binding tape. Insignificant as they were, Bartley offered to carry them to the wagon for her. Dorothy declined his offer and took them to the wagon herself.

"Now for that rifle," said Bartley.

Little Jim, itching all over to get hold of that new and shining weapon, squirmed as Hodges took it from the window and handed it to Bartley. Bartley examined it and passed it over to Little Jim.

"Is that the kind you wanted?" he asked.

"This is her! Twenty-two, long or short, genuwine repeater." Jimmy pretended to read the tags tied to the trigger guard. "Yep! This is her."

"And some cartridges," suggested Bartley.

"How many?" queried the storekeeper.

"All you got," said Little Jim.

But Bartley's good nature was not to be imposed upon to that extent. "Give us five boxes, Mr. Hodges."

"That cleans me out of twenty-twos," declared Hodges.

Jimmy grinned triumphantly. Dorothy had come in and was viewing the purchase with some apprehension. She knew Little Jim.

Bearing the rifle proudly, Jimmy marched from the store. Dorothy and Bartley followed him, and Bartley briefly outlined Cheyenne's recent sprightly exodus from San Andreas.

"I heard about it, from Mr. Hodges," said Dorothy. "And I also noticed that you have hurt your hand."

Bartley glanced at his right hand—and then at Dorothy, who was gazing at him curiously. It had become common news in town that Cheyenne Hastings and the Easterner had engaged in a free-for-all fight with the Sneed outfit, and that two of the Sneed boys were laid up for repairs. That was Mr. Hodges' version.

"I also heard that you had left town," said Dorothy.

Bartley's egoism was slightly deflated. Then Dorothy had come to town to buy a few trinkets, and not to find out how it fared with him.

"We have to get back before dark," she declared.

"And you got to drive," said Little Jim. "I want to try my new gun!"

"Did you thank Mr. Bartley for the gun?"

Little Jim admitted that he had forgotten to do so. He stuck out his small hand. "Thanks, pardner," he said heartily.

Bartley laughed and patted Jimmy's shoulder—something that Jimmy utterly detested, but suffered nobly, under the circumstances.

"You earned that gun—and thank you for fetching Miss Dorry to town."

"Huh! I didn't fetch *her*. She fetched me. Uncle Frank was comin', but Dorry said she just had to get some things—"

"Jimmy, please don't point that gun at the horses."

Bartley felt better. He didn't know just why he felt better. Yet he felt more than grateful to Little Jim.

Nevertheless, Dorothy met Bartley's eyes frankly as he said farewell. "I hope you will find time to ride over to the ranch," she said. "I'm sure Aunt Jane would be glad to see you."

"Thanks. Say, day after to-morrow?"

"Oh, it doesn't matter. Aunt Jane is nearly always at home."

"And I got lots of ca'tridges," chirruped Little Jim. "We can shoot all day."

"I wouldn't miss such an opportunity for anything," declared Bartley, yet he was looking at Dorothy when he spoke.

CHAPTER XX

ALONG THE FOOTHILLS

Bartley, enjoying his after-dinner smoke, felt that he wanted to know more about the girl who had invited him to call at the Lawrence ranch again. He told himself that he wanted to study her; to find out her preferences, her ideals, her attitude toward life, and how the thought of always living in the San Andreas Valley, shut away from the world, appealed to her.

With the unconscious intolerance of the city-bred man, he did not realize that her world was quite as interesting to her as his world was to him. Manlike, he also failed to realize that Dorothy was studying him quite as much as he was studying her. While he did not feel in the least superior, he did feel that he was more worldly-wise than this young woman whose horizon was bounded by the hills edging the San Andreas Valley.

True, she seemed to have read much, for one as isolated as she, and she had evidently appreciated what she had read. And then there was something about her that interested him, aside from her good looks. He had known many girls far more beautiful. It was not her manner, which was a bit constrained, at times. Her charm for him was indefinable. Somehow, she seemed different from other girls he had met. Bartley was himself responsible for this romantic hallucination. He saw her with eyes hungry for the sympathetic companionship of youth, especially feminine youth, for he could talk with her seriously about things which the genial Cheyenne could hardly appreciate.

In other words, Bartley, whose aim was to isolate himself from convention, was unconsciously hungry for the very conventions he thought he was fleeing from. And in a measure, Dorothy Gray represented the life he had left behind. Had she been a boy, Bartley would have enjoyed talking with her—or him; but she was a girl, and, concluded Bartley, just the type of girl for the heroine of a Western romance. Bartley's egoism would not allow him to admit that their tentative friendship could become anything more than friendship. And it was upon that understanding with himself that he saddled up, next morning,—why the hurry, with a week to spend in San Andreas,—and set out for the Lawrence ranch, to call on Aunt Jane.

Purposely he timed his arrival to follow the dinner hour—dinner was at noon in the ranch country—and was mildly lectured by Aunt Jane for not arriving earlier. Uncle Frank was at the lower end of the ranch, superintending the irrigating. Little Jim was on the veranda, needlessly cleaning his new rifle, preparatory to a rabbit hunt that afternoon. Bartley was at once invited to participate in the hunt, and he could think of no reason to decline. Dorothy, however, was not at the ranch.

Little Jim scrubbed his rifle with an oily rag, and scowled. "Got both hosses saddled, and lots of ca'tridges—and Dorry ain't here yet! She promised to be here right after dinner."

"Was Miss Dorry going with you?"

Jimmy nodded. "You bet! She's goin' to take my old twenty-two. It's only a single-shot," added Jimmy scornfully. "But it's good enough for a girl."

"Isn't it early to hunt rabbits?" queried Bartley.

"Sure! But we got to get there, clear over to the flats. If Dorry don't come as soon as I get this gun cleaned, I'm goin' anyhow."

But Dorothy appeared before Jimmy could carry out his threat of leaving without her. Jimmy, mounted on his pony, fretted to be gone, while Dorothy chatted a minute or so with Aunt Jane and Bartley. Finally they rode off, with Jimmy in the lead, explaining that there would be no rabbits on the flat until at least five o'clock, and in the meantime they would ride over to the spring and pretend they were starving. That is, Dorothy and Bartley were to pretend they were starving, while Jimmy scouted for meat and incidentally shot a couple of Indians and returned with a noble buck deer hanging across the saddle.

It was hot and they rode slowly. Far ahead, in the dim southern distances, lay the hills that walled the San Andreas Valley from the desert.

Dorothy noticed that Bartley gazed intently at those hills. "Cheyenne?" she queried, smiling.

"I beg your pardon. I was dreaming. Yes, I was thinking of him, and—" Bartley gestured toward Little Jim.

"Then you know?"

"Cheyenne told me, night before last, in San Andreas."

"Of course, Jimmy is far better off right where he is," asserted Dorothy, although Bartley had said nothing. "I don't think Cheyenne will ever settle down. At least, not so long as that man Sears is alive. Of course, if anything happens to Sears—"

Dorothy was interrupted by Little Jim, who turned in the saddle to address her. "Say, Dorry, if you keep on talkin' out loud, the Injuns is like to jump us! Scoutin' parties don't keep talkin' when they're on the trail."

"Don't be silly, Jimmy," laughed Dorothy.

"Well, they *used* to be Injuns in these hills, once."

"We'll behave," said Bartley. "But can't we ride toward the foothills and get in the shade?"

"You just follow me," said Little Jim. "I know this country."

It was Little Jim's day. It was his hunt. Dorothy and Bartley were merely his guests. He had allowed them to come with him—possibly because he wanted an audience. Presently Little Jim reined his horse to the left and rode up a dim trail among the boulders. By an exceedingly devious route he led the way to the spring, meanwhile playing the scout with intense concentration on some cattle tracks which were at least a month old. Bartley recognized the spot. Cheyenne and he had camped there upon their quest for the stolen horses. Little Jim assured his charges that all was safe, and he suggested that they "light down and rest a spell."

The contrasting coolness of the shade was inviting. Jimmy explained that there would be no rabbits visible until toward evening. Below and beyond them stretched the valley floor, shimmering in the sun. Behind them the hills rose and dipped, rose and dipped again, finally reaching up to the long slope of the mother range. Far above a thin, dark line of timber showed against the eastern sky.

"Ole Clubfoot Sneed lives up there," asserted Jimmy, pointing toward the distant ridge. "I been up there."

"Yes. And your father saved you from a whipping. Uncle Frank was very angry."

"I got that new rifle, anyhow," declared Little Jim.

"And they lived happily ever afterward," said Bartley.

"Huh! That's just like them fairy stories that Dorry reads to me sometimes. I like stories about Buffalo Bill and Injuns and fights. Fairy stories make me tired."

"Jimmy thinks he is quite grown up," teased Dorothy.

"You ain't growed up yourself, anyhow," retorted Jimmy. "Girls ain't growed up till they git married."

Dorothy turned to Bartley and began to talk about books and writers. Little Jim frowned. Why couldn't they talk about something worth listening to? Jimmy examined his new rifle, sighting it at different objects, and opening and closing the empty magazine. Finally he loaded it. His companions of the hunt were deep in a discussion having to do with Western stories. Jimmy fidgeted under the constant stress of keeping silent. He would have interrupted Dorothy, willingly enough, but Bartley's presence rather awed him.

Jimmy felt that his afternoon was being wasted. However, there was the solace of the new rifle, and plenty of ammunition. While he knew there was no big game in those hills, he could pretend that there was. He debated with himself as to whether he would hunt deer, bear, or mountain lion. Finally he decided he would hunt bear. He waited for an opportunity to leave without being noticed, and, carrying his trusty rifle at the ready, he stealthily disappeared in the brush south of the spring. A young boy, with a new gun and lots of brush to prowl through! Under such circumstances the optimist can imagine anything from rabbits to elephants.

Some time passed before Dorothy missed him. She called. There was no reply. "He won't go far," she assured Bartley who rose to go and look for Jimmy.

Bartley sat down by the spring again. He questioned Dorothy in regard to ranch life, social conditions, local ambitions, and the like. Quite impersonally she answered him, explaining that the folk in the valley were quite content, so long as they were moderately successful. Of course, the advent of that funny little machine, the automobile, would revolutionize ranch life, eventually. Why, a wealthy rancher of San Andreas had actually driven to Los Angeles and back in one of those little machines!

Bartley smiled. "They've come to stay, no doubt. But I can't reconcile automobiles with saddle-horses and buckboards. I shan't have an automobile snorting and snuffing through my story."

"Your story!"

"I really didn't mean to speak about it. But the cat is out of the bag. I'm making notes for a Western novel, Miss Gray. I confess it."

"Confession usually implies having done something wrong, doesn't it?"

Henry Herbert Knibbs

"Yes. But with you as the heroine of my story, I couldn't go very far wrong."

Dorothy flushed and bit her lip. So that was why Bartley had been so attentive and polite? He had been studying her, questioning her, mentally jotting down what she had said—and he had not told her, until that moment, that he was writing a story. She had not known that he was a writer of stories.

"You might, at least, have asked me if I cared to be a Western heroine in your story."

"Oh, that would have spoiled it all! Can't you see? You would not have been yourself, if you had known. And our visits—"

"I don't think I care to be the heroine of your story, Mr. Bartley."

"You really mean it?"

Dorothy nodded thoughtfully. Bartley knew, intuitively, that she was sincere—that she was not angling for flattery. He had thought that he was rather paying her a compliment in making her the heroine of his first Western book; or, at least, that she would take it as a compliment. He frowned, twisting a spear of dry grass in his fingers.

"Of course—that needn't make any difference about your calling—on Aunt Jane."

"Thank you," laughed Bartley. "And because of the privilege which I really appreciate, I'll agree to look for another heroine."

Dorothy had not expected just such an answer. "In San Andreas?" she queried.

"I can't say. I'll be lucky if I find another, anywhere, to compare—"

"If you had asked me, first," interrupted Dorothy, "I might have said 'yes.'"

"I'm sorry I didn't. Won't you reconsider?"

Dorothy shook her head. Then she looked up at him frankly, steadily. "I think you took me for granted. That is what I didn't like."

"But—I didn't! It didn't occur to me to really begin my story until after I had seen you. Of course I knew I would write a new story sooner or later. I hope you will believe that."

"Yes. But I think I know why you decided to stay in San Andreas, instead of riding south, with Cheyenne. Aunt Jane and Little Jim and your heroine were within easy riding distance."

"I'll admit I intended to write about Aunt Jane and Jimmy. I actually adore Aunt Jane. And Little Jim, he's what one might call an unknown quantity—"

"He seems to be, just now."

"Oh, he won't go far," said Bartley, smiling.

Dorothy tossed her head. "And Cheyenne—"

"Oh, he is the moving figure in the story. That is not a pun, if you please. I had no idea that Cheyenne could actually hate any one, until the other night when he told me about—Laramie, and that man Sears."

"Did he talk much about Sears?"

"Not much—but enough. Frankly, I think Cheyenne will kill Sears if he happens to meet him again."

"And that will furnish the climax for your story!" said Dorothy scornfully.

"Well, if it has to happen—" Bartley paused.

Dorothy's face was troubled. Finally she rose and picked up her gloves and hat.

"I wish some one or something would stop him," she said slowly. "He liked you. All the years he has been riding up and down the country he has ridden alone, until he met you. I'm sorry you didn't go with him."

"He did pretend that he was disappointed when I told him I was going to stay in San Andreas for a while."

"You thought he was joking, but he wasn't. We have all tried to get him to settle down; but he would not listen. If I were a man—"

"Then you think I could have influenced him?" queried Bartley.

"You might have tried, at least."

"Well, he's gone. And I'll have to make the best of it—and also find another heroine," said Bartley lightly, trying to make her smile.

"I'll be the heroine of your story, upon one condition," Dorothy said, finally.

"And that is—"

"If you will try and find Cheyenne and—and just be a friend to him. I suppose it sounds silly, and I would not think of asking you to try and keep him from doing anything he decided to do. But you might happen to be able to say the right word at the right time."

"I hardly took myself as seriously as that, in connection with Cheyenne," declared Bartley. "I suppose, if I should saddle up and ride south to-morrow, I might overtake him along the road, somewhere. He travels slowly."

"But you won't go, just because I spoke as I did?"

"Not altogether because of that. I like Cheyenne."

Impetuously Dorothy stepped close to Bartley and laid her hand on his arm. "I knew you were like that! And what does writing about people amount to, when you can really do something for them? It isn't just Cheyenne. There's Little Jim—"

"Yes. But where *is* Little Jim?"

Dorothy called in her high, clear voice. There was no answering halloo. "His horse is there. I can't understand—"

"I'll look around a bit," said Bartley. "He's probably ambushing us, somewhere, and expects us to be tremendously surprised."

"I'll catch up my horse," said Dorothy. "No, you had better

let me catch him. He knows me."

And Dorothy stepped from the clearing round the spring and walked toward the horses. They were grazing quite a ways off, up the hillside.

Bartley recalled having glimpsed Little Jim crawling through the brush on the south side of the spring. No doubt Jimmy had grown tired of waiting, and had dropped down to the mesa on foot to hunt rabbits. Once clear of the hillside brush, Bartley was able to overlook the mesa below. Presently he discerned a black hat moving along slowly. Evidently the young hunter was stalking game.

Bartley hesitated to call out. He doubted that Jimmy could hear him at that distance. Stepping down the gentle slope of the hillside to the road, Bartley watched Jimmy for a while, hoping that he would turn and see him. But Jimmy was busy. "Might as well go back and get the horses and ride over to him," said Bartley.

He had turned to cross the road, when he heard the sound of quick hoof-beats. Surely Dorothy had not caught up the horses so soon? Bartley turned toward the bend of the road. Presently a rider, his worn chaps flapping, his shapeless hat pulled low, and his quirt swinging at every jump of the horse, pounded up and had almost passed Bartley, when he set up his horse and dismounted. Bartley did not recognize him until he spoke.

"My name's Hull. I was lookin' for you."

"All right, Mr. Hull. What do you want?"

Hull's gaze traveled up and down the Easterner. Hull was looking to see if the other carried a gun. Bartley expected argument and inwardly braced himself. Meanwhile he wondered if he could find Hull's chin again, and as easily as he had found it that night back of the livery barn. Hull loomed big and heavy, and it was evident from the minute he dismounted that he meant business.

Without a word, Hull swung at Bartley, smashing in with right and left, fighting like a wild-cat, forcing his weight into the fight, and kicking wickedly when he got a chance. Finally, after taking a straight blow in the face, Hull clinched—and the minute Bartley felt those tough-sinewed arms around him he knew that he was in for a licking.

Bartley's only chance, and that a pretty slim one, lay in getting free from the grip of those arms. He used his knee effectively. Hull grunted and staggered back. Bartley jumped forward and bored in, knocking Hull off his feet. The cow-puncher struck the ground, rolled over, and was up and coming like a cyclone. It flashed through Bartley's mind that the only thing to do was to stay with it till the finish. Hull was beating him down slowly, but surely.

Dully conscious that some one was calling, behind him, Bartley struck out, straight and clean, but he might as well have tried to stop a runaway freight with a whisk-broom. He felt the smashing impact of a blow—then suddenly he was on his back in the road—and he had no desire to get up. Free from the hammering of those heavy fists, he felt compa- ratively comfortable.

"You brute!" It was Dorothy's voice, tense with anger.

Bartley heard another voice, thick with heavy breathing. "That's all right, Miss Gray. But the dude had it comin'."

Then Bartley heard the sound of hoof-beats—and somehow

or other, Dorothy was helping him to his feet. He tried to grin—but his lips would not obey his will.

"I'm all right," he mumbled.

"Perhaps," said Dorothy, steady and cool. "But you'll want to wash your face at the spring. I fetched your horse."

"Lord, Miss Gray, let's walk. I'm more used to it."

"It was that man Hull, from the mountain, wasn't it?"

"I don't know his name. I *did* meet him once, in San Andreas, after dark."

"I'll just tie the horses, here. It's not far to the spring. Feel dizzy?"

"A little. But I can walk without help, thank you. Little Jim is down there, stalking rabbits."

At the spring Bartley knelt and washed the blood from his face and felt tenderly of his half closed eye, twisted his neck round and felt a sharp click—and then his head became clearer. His light shirt was half-torn from his shoulders, and he was scandalously mussed up, to put it mildly. He got to his feet and faced Dorothy.

"There's a formula for this sort of thing, in books," he said. "Just now I can't recall it. First, however, you say you're 'all right,' if you are alive. If you are not, it doesn't matter. Then you say, 'a mere scratch!' But I'm certain of one thing. I never needed a heroine more than I did when you arrived."

Dorothy smiled in spite of herself. "You aren't pretending, are you? I mean—about your condition?"

"I should say not. My eye is closed. My right arm won't work, and my head feels queer—and I am *not* hungry. But my soul goes marching on."

"Then we'll have to find Jimmy. It's getting late."

CHAPTER XXI

"GIT ALONG CAYUSE"

It was dark when Bartley arrived at his hotel in San Andreas. Not caring to parade his black eye and his swollen mouth, he took his evening meal at a little Mexican restaurant, and then went back to his room, where he spent the evening adding a few more pertinent notes to his story; notes that were fresh in his mind. He knew what it felt like to take a good licking. In fact, the man is unfortunate who does not. Bartley thought he could write effectively upon the subject.

He had found Dorothy's quiet sympathy rather soothing. She had made no fuss whatever about the matter. And she had not insisted that he stop at the ranch and get doctored up. Little Jim had promptly asked Bartley, "Who done it?" and Bartley had told him. Little Jim asked more questions and was silenced only by a promise from Dorothy to buy him more cartridges. "That is, if you promise not to say anything about it to Aunt Jane or Uncle Frank," she stipulated. Little Jim gravely shook hands upon the agreement. Dorothy knew that he would keep his word.

This agreement had been made after Bartley had left them. Dorothy had sworn Little Jim to silence, not so much on Bartley's account as on her own. Should the news of the fight become public, there would be much bucolic comment, wherein her name would be mentioned and the whole affair interpreted to suit the crude imaginings of the community. Bartley also realized this and, because of it, stuck close to his room for two days, meanwhile making copious notes for the new story.

But the making of notes for the story was a rather tame occupation compared with the possibilities of actual adventure on the road. He had a good saddle-horse, plenty of optimism, and enough money to pay his way wherever he chose to go. Incidentally he had a notebook and pencil. What more did a man need to make life worth while?

And then, somewhere along the southern highway Cheyenne was jogging with Filaree and Joshua:

> Seems like I don't git anywhere:
> Git along, cayuse, git along.

Bartley rose and stepped to the window. San Andreas drowsed in the noon sun. Far to the north he could see a dot of fresh green—the cottonwoods of the Lawrence rancho. Again he found himself in the grip of indecision. After all, a fellow didn't have to journey up and down the land to find material for a story. There was plenty of material right where he was. All he had to do was to stop, look, and listen. "Hang the story!" he exclaimed peevishly. "I'll just go out and *live*—and then write the story."

It did not take him long to pack his saddle-bags, nor to get together the few articles of clothing he had had washed by a Mexican woman in town. He wrote a brief note to Dorothy, stating that he was on his way. He paid his hotel bill, stepped round to the livery and paid for Dobe's entertainment, saddled up, and, literally shaking the dust of San Andreas from his feet, rode down the long trail south, headed for Joe Scott's placer, as his first stop.

He would spend the night there and then head south again. The only living thing that seemed interested in Bartley's exodus was a stray dog that seemed determined to follow him. Turning from the road, Bartley took the short cut to Scott's placer. Glancing back he saw that the dog was still following. Bartley told him to go home. The dog, a very ordinary yellow dog, didn't happen to have a home—and he was hungry. So he ignored Bartley's command.

Whether or not he imagined that Bartley was different from the run of townsfolk is a question. Possibly he imagined Bartley might give him something to eat. In any event, the dog stuck to the trail clear up to Scott's placer.

Scott was not at the cabin. Bartley hallooed, glanced round, and dismounted. On the cabin door was a note: "Gone to Phoenix. J. Scott."

Bartley turned from the cabin to find the dog gazing up at him mournfully; his expression seemed to convey the idea that they were both in hard luck. Nobody home and nothing to eat.

"What, you here!" exclaimed Bartley.

The yellow dog wagged his tail. He was young and as yet had some faith in mankind.

Bartley tied his horse and strode up the trail to the workings. Everything had been put in order. The dog helped investigate, sniffing at the wheelbarrow, the buckets, the empty sacks weighted down with rock to keep them from blowing away, the row of tools, picks and shovels and bars. Evidently the owner of the place was not concealed beneath any of these things.

Meanwhile the afternoon shadows warned Bartley that a camp with water and feed was the next thing in order. He strode back to the cabin. There was no problem to solve, although he thought there was. The yellow dog, an old campaigner in the open, though young in years, solved his problem by a suggestion. He was tired. There seemed to be no food in sight. He philosophically trotted to the open shed opposite the cabin and made a bed for himself in a pile of gunny-sacks. Bartley grinned. Why not?

Experience had taught Bartley to carry something else, besides a notebook and pencil, in his saddle-bags. Hence the crackers and can of corned beef came in handy. The mountain water was cold and refreshing. There was hay in the burro stable. Moreover, Bartley now had a happy companion who licked his chops, wagged his tail, and grinned as he finished a bit of corned beef. Bartley tossed him a cracker. The dog caught it and it disappeared. This was something like it! Here was a man who rode a big horse, didn't kick stray dogs, and even shared a meal with a fellow! Such a man was worth following forever.

"It would seem that you have adopted me," declared Bartley. The dog had shown no inclination to leave since being fed. There might possibly be another meal coming, later.

"But what am I going to do with you?" queried Bartley, as the dog curled up on the pile of gunny-sacks. "You don't look as though you habitually stopped at hotels, and I'll have to, until I catch up with Cheyenne. What's the answer?"

The yellow dog, all snuggled down in the sacks, peered at Bartley with unblinking eyes. Bartley laughed. Then he made his own bed with gunny-sacks, and after smoking a cigarette, turned in and slept well.

He did not expect to find the dog there in the morning. But the dog was there, most evidently waiting for breakfast, grinning his delight at not being cursed or kicked at, and frisking round the cabin yard in a mad race after nothing in particular, and indicating in every way possible that he was the happiest dog that ever wagged a tail.

Crackers and corned beef again, and spring water for breakfast. And while Dobe munched his hay, Bartley smoked and roughly planned his itinerary. He would travel south as far as Phoenix and then swing back again, over the old Apache Trail—if he did not overtake Cheyenne.

If he did overtake him, the plan might be changed. It did not matter. He had set out to find his erstwhile traveling companion. If he found him, they could just as well travel together. If he did not, Bartley determined to see much of the country. In so far as influencing Cheyenne in any way—that would have to be determined by chance. Bartley felt that his influence with the sprightly Cheyenne weighed very little against Cheyenne's hatred for Panhandle Sears.

Once more upon the road, with the early morning shadows slanting across the valley, Bartley felt that it was his own fault if he did not enjoy himself. Swinging into an easy trot he turned to see if the yellow dog were following him. At first Bartley thought the dog had shown wisdom and had departed for San Andreas, but, happening to glance down on the other side of his horse, he saw the dog trotting along, close to Dobe's heels.

Bartley felt a pity for the dog's dumb, insistent attachment. Reining in, Bartley told the dog he had better go home. For answer the dog lay down in the horse's shadow, his head on his paws, and his eyes fixed on Bartley's face. He did not seem to know what the words meant. But he did know—only pretended he did not. His rooftree was the Arizona sky, and his home the place where his adopted master camped at night.

"Oh, very well," said Bartley, smiling in spite of himself.

That noon they stopped at a ranch where Bartley had dinner and fed his horse. Cheyenne had passed that way several days ago, the ranch folk told him. It was about twenty miles to the next town. Bartley was invited to stop by and spend the night, but he declined the invitation, even as they had declined to accept money for their hospitality. Meanwhile the dog had disappeared. He had not followed Bartley into the ranch. And it was some twenty minutes or so after Bartley was on the road again that he discovered the dog, coming round a bend on the run. There was no getting rid of him.

The dog, who had often been chased from ranches by other dogs, had at first waited patiently for Bartley to appear. Then, as Bartley did not appear, the dog made a short scout through the near-by brush. Finally he stirred up a rabbit. It was a long, hard chase, but the dog got his dinner. Then, circling, he took up Bartley's trail from the ranch, overtaking him with grim determination not to lose sight of him again.

Arriving at the town of Stacey early that afternoon, Bartley arranged with the local liveryman for the dog's keep that night. From that night on, the dog never let Dobe out of his sight. It was evidently intended that he should sleep in stalls and guard Dobe against the approach of any one save his master.

Bartley learned that Cheyenne had passed through Stacey headed south. He had stopped at the local store to purchase provisions. Estimating roughly, Bartley was making better time than had Cheyenne, yet it would be several days before he could possibly overtake him.

Next day Bartley had ridden better than forty miles, and that night he stayed at a ranch, where he was made welcome. In fact, any one who rode a good horse and appeared to be even halfway civil never suffered for want of a meal or a bed in those days. Gasoline has somewhat diluted such hospitality, yet there are sections of Arizona still unspoiled, where the stranger is made to feel that the word "home" has retained its ancient and honorable significance.

CHAPTER XXII

BOX-S BUSINESS

A few days later, Bartley stopped at a small town to have his horse shod. The blacksmith seemed unusually interested in the horse and complimented Bartley upon owning such a good mount.

"Comes from up San Andreas way," said the smith, noticing the brand on Dobe's flank.

"Yes. I picked him up at Antelope. I understand he was raised on Senator Brown's ranch."

"That's Steve Brown's brand, all right. Heard the news from up that way?"

"Nothing special."

"Seems somebody run off a bunch of Senator Steve's horses, last week. Thought mebby you'd heard."

"No."

"Well, thought I'd just tell you. I seen one posse ride through yesterday. They'll be lookin' for strangers along the road."

"Thanks. I bought this horse—and I happen to know Senator Brown."

"No offense, stranger. If I'd 'a' suspicioned you'd stole that horse, you wouldn't take him out of here. Like I said to Cheyenne, last week; he could fetch a whole carload of stock in here and take 'em out again without trouble. He was tellin' me how he lost his horses, and we got to talkin' about some folks bein' blind when they're facin' a brand on a critter. Mebby you heard tell of Cheyenne Hastings?"

"I have traveled with him. You say he stopped here a few days ago?"

"Well, not just stopped; he kind of looked in to see how I was gettin' along. He acted queerlike, for him. I've knowed Cheyenne for years. Said he was feelin' all right. He ast me if I'd seen Panhandle Sears down this way, recent. Seemed kind of disappointed when I told him no. Cheyenne used to be a right-smart man, before he had trouble with that woman of his."

"Yes? He told me about it," said Bartley, not caring to hear any more of the details of Cheyenne's trouble.

"'Most everybody knows it," stated the smith. "And if I was Sears I'd sure leave this country."

"So should I. I've seen Cheyenne handle a gun."

"You got the right idea!" exclaimed the blacksmith, evidently pleased. "All Cheyenne's friends have been waitin' for years for him to clean that slate and start fresh again. He used to be a right-smart hand, before he had trouble."

The blacksmith accompanied his conversation with considerable elbow motion and the rattle and clang of shaping horseshoes. Presently Dobe was new shod and ready for the road. Bartley paid the smith, thanked him for a good job, and rode south. Evidently Cheyenne's open quarrel with Sears was the talk of the countryside. It was expected of Cheyenne that he would "clean the slate and start fresh" some day. And cleaning the slate meant killing Sears. To Bartley it seemed strange that any one should be pleased with the idea of one man killing another deliberately.

In speaking of the recent horse-stealings, the blacksmith had mentioned no names. But Bartley at once drew the conclusion that it had been Sneed's men who had run off the Senator's horses. Sneed was known to be a horse-thief. He had never been convicted, although he had been arrested and tried several times. It was also known that Senator Steve had openly vowed that he would rid the country of Sneed, sooner or later.

Several times, during his journey south, Bartley was questioned, but never interfered with. Thus far he heard of Cheyenne occasionally, but, nearing Phoenix, he lost track of his erstwhile companion. However, he took it for granted that Phoenix had been Cheyenne's destination. And Bartley wanted to see the town for himself, in any event.

*   *   *   *   *

Cheyenne, arriving in Phoenix, stabled his horses at the Top-Notch livery, and took a room for himself directly opposite the Hole-in-the-Wall gambling-house. He refused to drink with the occasional acquaintance he met, not because he did not like liquor, but because Colonel Stevenson, the city marshal, had told him that Panhandle Sears and his friends were in town.

"Why don't you tell me to go git him?" queried Cheyenne,

Henry Herbert Knibbs

looking the marshal in the eye.

"I didn't think it was necessary," said the marshal.

"What? To git him?"

The marshal smiled. Then casually: "I hear that Panhandle and his friends are drinking heavy and spending considerable money. They must have made a strike, somewhere."

"I see by the paper somebody run off a bunch of the Box-S hosses," remarked Cheyenne, also casually.

Then, without further comment, he left the marshal wondering if Panhandle's presence in town had any connection with the recent running-off of the Box-S stock. The sheriff of Antelope had wired Colonel Stevenson to be on the lookout for Bill Sneed and his gang, but had not mentioned Panhandle's name in the telegram.

The following day, Senator Brown and his foreman, Lon Pelly, arrived in Phoenix and had a long talk with the marshal. That afternoon Lon Pelly took the train south. Early in the evening Senator Brown received a telegram from Pelly stating that Sneed and four men had left Tucson, headed north and riding horses.

The stolen horses had been trailed south as far as Phoenix. It was evident that they had been driven to Tucson and disposed of somewhere in that vicinity. Yet there was no conclusive proof that Sneed had stolen the horses. As usual, he had managed to keep a few days ahead of his pursuers. Sneed was known to have left his camp in the hills above San Andreas. The first posse had found the camp abandoned. Sneed had not been identified until Pelly got track of him in Tucson.

During his talk with Senator Brown the marshal mentioned the fact that Panhandle Sears was in Phoenix.

"Did Panhandle come in from the south?" queried the Senator.

"Nobody seems to know."

"Well, if he did, we have got the link that's missing in this chain, Colonel. Pelly is holdin' one end of the chain down in Tucson, and the other end is layin' right here in Phoenix. If we can connect her up—"

"But we haven't located the horses, Senator."

"Colonel, I'll find those horses if I can. But I'm after Sneed, this journey. He has been running things about ten years too long to suit me. I've got a check-book with me. You have the men. I'm out to do a little housecleanin' of my own. If we can get Panhandle to talk, we can find out something."

"He's been on a drunk for a week. I could run him in for disturbing the peace and—"

"And he'd suspect what we're after and freeze up, tight. No, let him run loose, but keep your eye on him. He'll give the deal away, sooner or later."

"I hope it's sooner," said the Colonel. "Cheyenne is holed up down the street, waiting for a chance to get Sears. Cheyenne didn't say so, but it was in his eye. He's changed considerable since I saw him last."

"Was there any one with him: a tall, dark-haired, kind of clean-cut boy, for instance?"

Henry Herbert Knibbs

"No, not when I saw him. He rode in with his usual outfit."

"Wonder where he lost young Bartley? Well, I'm glad the boy isn't here. He might get hurt."

"Wild?"

"No. Quiet. Writes stories. He's out here to look at the West. Stayed at the ranch a spell. Mrs. Brown likes him."

Colonel Stevenson nodded and offered the Senator a cigar. "Let's step over to the hotel, Steve. It's a long time since—"

* * * * *

That evening Bartley arrived in Phoenix, put up his horse, and, upon inquiry, learned that the Grand Central was the best hotel in town. He was registering when he noticed Senator Brown's name. He made inquiry of the clerk. Yes, the Senator had arrived that morning. And would Mr. Bartley prefer a front room? The front rooms on the north side were cooler. No, the clerk knew nothing about a Mr. Cheyenne. There was no one by that name registered at the hotel. It was past the regular dinner hour, but the dining-room was not yet closed. There was a men's furnishings store just across the street. They carried a complete stock. And did Mr. Bartley wish to be called at any special hour in the morning? Breakfast was served from six-thirty to nine-thirty.

Bartley had dinner, and later strolled around to the Top-Notch livery to see that Dobe was being well cared for. While talking with the stableman, Bartley noticed a gray pony and in the next stall a buckskin—Cheyenne's horses.

"Those are Cheyenne's horses, aren't they?" he queried.

"I dunno. Mebby that's his name. He left 'em here a few days ago. I only seen him once, since then."

"I'll be around in the morning. If a man called Cheyenne should happen to come in, just tell him that Bartley is stopping at the Grand Central."

"I'll tell him, all right," said the stableman.

And as soon as Bartley was out of sight, that worthy called up the city marshal and told him that a stranger had ridden in and stabled a horse bearing the Box-S brand. A big reward had been offered for the stolen horses.

At the hotel Bartley learned that Senator Brown had gone out for the evening. Tired from his long ride, Bartley went to his room. Senator Steve and Cheyenne were in town. Bartley recalled the blacksmith's talk about the stolen horses. No doubt that accounted for Senator Steve's presence in Phoenix. As for Cheyenne—Bartley decided to hunt him up in the morning.

CHAPTER XXIII

THE HOLE-IN-THE-WALL

Panhandle Sears, in a back room in the Hole-in-the-Wall, was ugly drunk. The Hole-in-the-Wall had the reputation of running a straight game. Whether or not the game was straight, Panhandle had managed to drop his share of the money from the sale of the Box-S horses. He had had nothing to do with the actual stealing of them, but he had, with the assistance of his Mexican companion Posmo, engineered the sale to a rancher living out of Tucson. It was understood that the horses would find their way across the border.

Now Panhandle was broke again. He stated that unpleasant fact to his companions, Posmo and Shorty,—the latter a town loafer he had picked up in Antelope. Shorty had nothing to say. Panhandle's drunken aggressive cowed him. But Posmo, who had really found the market for the stolen stock, felt that he had been cheated. Panhandle had promised him a third of his share of the money. Panhandle had kept on promising from day to day, liquidating his promises with whiskey. And now there was no money.

Posmo knew Panhandle well enough not to press the matter, just then. But Panhandle, because neither of his companions had said anything when told that he was broke, turned on Posmo.

"What you got to say about it, anyway?" he asked with that curious stubbornness born in liquor.

"I say that you owe me a hundred dollar," declared Posmo.

"Well, go ahead and collect!"

"Yes, go ahead and collect," said Shorty, suddenly siding with Panhandle. "We blowed her in. We're broke, but we ain't cryin' about it."

"That is all right," said Posmo quietly. "If the money is gone, she is gone; yes?"

"That's the way to say it!" asserted Panhandle, changing front and slapping Posmo on the shoulder. "We're broke, and who the hell cares?"

"Let's have a drink," suggested Shorty. "I got a couple of beans left."

They slouched out from the back room and stood at the bar. Panhandle immediately became engaged in noisy argument with one of the frequenters of the place. Senator Brown's name was mentioned by the other, but mentioned casually, with no reference whatever to stolen horses.

Panhandle laughed. "So old Steve is down here lookin' for his hosses, eh?"

"What horses?"

The question, spoken by no one knew whom, chilled the

group to silence.

Panhandle saw that he had made a blunder. "Who wants to know?" he queried, gazing round the barroom.

"Why, it's in all the papers," declared the bartender conciliatingly. "The Box-S horses was run off a couple of weeks ago."

Panhandle turned his back on the group and called for a drink.

Shorty was tugging gently at his sleeve. "Posmo's beat it, Pan."

"To hell with him! Beat it yourself if you feel like it."

"I'll stick Pan," declared Shorty, yet his furtive eyes belied his assertion.

*   *   *   *   *

For three days Bartley had tried to find where Cheyenne was staying, but without success, chiefly because Cheyenne kept close to his room during the daytime, watching the entrance to the Hole-in-the-Wall, waiting for Panhandle to step out into the daylight, when there would be folk on the street who could witness that Panhandle had drawn his gun first. Cheyenne determined to give his enemy that chance, and then kill him. But thus far Panhandle had not appeared on the street in the daytime, so far as Cheyenne knew.

Incidentally, Senator Steve had warned Bartley to keep away from the Hole-in-the-Wall district after dark, intimating that there was more in the wind than Cheyenne's feud with Panhandle Sears. So Bartley contented himself with acting as a sort of private secretary for the Senator, a duty that was a pleasure. The hardest thing Bartley did was to refuse bottled entertainment, at least once out of every three times it was offered.

On the evening of the fourth day after Pelly had wired the Senator that Sneed and his men had ridden north from Tucson, Posmo, hanging about the eastern outskirts of Phoenix, saw a small band of horsemen against the southern sky-line. Knowing the trail they would take, north, Posmo had timed their arrival almost to the hour. They would pass to the east of Phoenix, and take the old Apache Trail, North. Posmo had his horse saddled and hidden in a draw. He mounted and rode directly toward the oncoming horsemen.

He sang as he rode. It was safer to do that, when it was growing dark. The riders would know he was a Mexican, and that he did not wish to conceal his identity on the road. He did not care to be mistaken for an enemy, especially so near Phoenix.

Sneed, a giant in the dusk, reined in as Posmo hailed the group. Sneed asked his name. Posmo replied, and was told to ride up. Sneed, separating himself from his men, rode a little ahead and met Posmo.

"Panhandle is give the deal away," stated Posmo.

"How?"

"He drunk and spend all the money. He do not give me anything for that I make the deal—over there," and Posmo gestured toward the south.

"Double-crossed you, eh? And now you're sore and want his scalp."

"He talk too much of the Box-S horses in that cantina," stated Posmo deliberately. "He say that you owe him money." This was an afterthought, and an invention.

"Who did he say that to?" queried Sneed.

"He tell everybody in that place that you turn the good trick and then throw him hard."

"Either you're lyin', or Panhandle's crazy." Sneed turned and called to his men, a few paces off. They rode up on tired horses. "What do you say, boys? Panhandle is talkin', over there in Phoenix. Posmo, here, says Panhandle is talkin' about us. Now nobody's got a thing on us. We been south lookin' at some stock we're thinkin' of buyin'. Want to ride over with me and have a little talk with Panhandle?"

"Ain't that kind of risky, Cap?"

"Every time! But it ain't necessary to ride right into the marshal's office. We put our little deal through clean. The horses we're ridin' belong to us. And who's goin' to stop us from ridin' in, or out, of town? I aim to talk to Panhandle into ridin' north with us. It's safer to have him along. If you all don't want to ride with me, I'll go in alone."

"We're with you, Cap," said one of the men.

"Mebby it's safer to ride through the towns from now on than to keep dodgin' 'em," suggested Lawson.

"Come on, then," and Sneed indicated Posmo.

"And don't make any mistakes," threatened Lawson, riding close to the Mexican. "If you do—you won't last."

Posmo had not counted on this turn of affairs. He had supposed that his news would send Sneed and his men in to have it out with Panhandle, or that one of them would ride in and persuade Panhandle to join them. But he now knew that he would have to ride with Sneed, or he would be suspected of double-dealing.

At the fork of the road leading into Phoenix, Sneed reined in. "We're ridin' tired horses, boys. And we ain't lookin' for trouble. All we want is Panhandle. We'll get him."

Sitting his big horse like a statue, his club foot concealed by the long *tapadero*, his physical being dominating his followers, Sneed headed the group that rode slowly down the long open stretch bordering on the east of the town. They entered town quietly and stopped a few doors below the lighted front of the Hole-in-the-Wall.

"Just step in and tell Panhandle I want to see him," and Sneed indicated one of his riders.

The man went in and came out again with the information that Panhandle had left the saloon about an hour ago; that he had told the bartender he was going out to get some money and come back and play the wheel.

"Get on your horse," said Sneed, who had been gazing up the street while listening to the other. "Here comes Panhandle now. I'll do the talking."

CHAPTER XXIV

CHEYENNE PLAYS BIG

Watching from his darkened window, Cheyenne had seen Panhandle leave the Hole-in-the-Wall, and stride up the street alone. It was the first time Cheyenne had seen Sears since he had taken the single room opposite the gambling-house. Cheyenne stepped back, drew down the curtain, and turned on the light. The bare board floor was littered with cigarette stubs. A pair of saddle-bags hung on the iron bedstead. Other furniture was a chair, a scratched and battered washstand, a cracked mirror. Standing by the washstand Cheyenne took his gun from its holster, half-cocked it, and punched out the loaded cartridges. He pulled the pin, pushed the cylinder out with his thumb, and examined it against the light. Carefully he cleaned and replaced the cylinder, reloaded it, held the hammer back, and spun the cylinder with his hand. Finally he thrust the gun in the holster and, striding to the bed, sat down, his chin in his hands.

Somewhere out there on the street, or in the Hole-in-the-Wall, he would meet his enemy—in a few minutes, perhaps. There would be no wordy argument. They understood each other, and had understood each other, since that morning, long ago when they had passed each other on the road—Panhandle riding in to Laramie and Cheyenne and Little Jim riding from the abandoned home. Cheyenne thought of Little Jim, of his wife, and, by some queer trick of mind, of Bartley. He knew that the Easterner was in town. The stableman at the Top-Notch had told him. Well, he had seen Panhandle. Now he would go out and meet him, or overtake him.

Some one turned from the street into the hall below and rapidly climbed the stairs. Cheyenne heard a knock at the door opposite his. That room was unoccupied. Then came a brisk knock at his own door.

"What do you want?"

"Is that you, Cheyenne?"

"Who wants to know?"

"Bartley. I just found out from Colonel Stevenson where you were camping."

Cheyenne stepped to the door and unlocked it.

Bartley entered, glanced round the room, and then shook hands with Cheyenne. "Been a week trying to find you. How are you and how are the horses? Man, but it was a long, lonesome ride from San Andreas! If it hadn't been for that dog that adopted me—by the way, Colonel Stevenson was telling Senator Brown that Panhandle is in town. I suppose you know it."

"I seen him, this evenin'."

"So did I. Just passed him as I came down here. The Colonel said you were camping somewhere opposite the Hole-in-the-Wall. How is everything?"

"Quiet."

"Were you going anywhere?"

"No place in particular."

Bartley sat down on the edge of the bed and lighted a cigarette. Cheyenne stood as though waiting for him to leave. There was something queer about Cheyenne. His eyes were somber, his manner stiff and unnatural. His greeting had been cool.

"About that man Panhandle—" Bartley began, but Cheyenne interrupted with a gesture.

"You say you saw him, on your way down here?"

"Yes. He didn't seem to recognize me. He was walking fast."

"How was Little Jim when you left?"

"Just fine!"

"And the folks?"

"Same as ever. Miss Gray—"

"Well, I reckon I'll be steppin' along. Glad I saw you again."

"Going to leave town to-night?"

"I aim to."

Bartley could no longer ignore Cheyenne's attitude. He knew that something had happened or was about to happen. Cheyenne's manner did not invite question or suggestion. Yet

Bartley had promised Dorothy that he would exert what influence he had—and it seemed a critical time, just at that moment.

"I'd like to talk with you a minute, if you have time," said Bartley.

"Won't do no good, pardner." And without waiting for Bartley to say anything more, Cheyenne stepped up to him and held out his hand. "So long," he said.

"Well, good luck!" replied Bartley, and shook hands with him heartily. "I hope you win."

Cheyenne gestured toward the door. Bartley stepped out into the hallway. The light in the room flickered out.

"I reckon you'll be goin' back to your hotel," said Cheyenne. "Wait. I'll just step down first."

At the foot of the stairs Cheyenne paused and glanced up and down the street. Directly across the way the Hole-in-the-Wall was ablaze with light. A few doors east of the gambling-hall an indistinct group of riders sat their horses as though waiting for some one. Cheyenne drew back into the shadows of the hallway.

Bartley peered out over Cheyenne's shoulder. From up the street in the opposite direction came the distant click of boot-heels. A figure strode swiftly toward the patch of white light in front of the gambling-hall.

"Just stand back a little, pardner," said Cheyenne.

Bartley felt his heart begin to thump as Cheyenne gently loosened his gun in the holster.

"It's Panhandle!" whispered Bartley, as the figure of Sears was silhouetted against the lighted windows of the place opposite.

Out of the shadows where the riders waited came a single, abrupt word, peremptory, incisive: "Panhandle!"

Panhandle, about to turn into the lighted doorway, stopped short.

Sneed had called to Panhandle; but it was Posmo the Mexican who rode forward to meet him. Sneed, close behind Posmo, watched to see that the Mexican carried out his instructions, which were simply to tell Panhandle to get his horse and leave town with them. Seeing the group behind the Mexican, Panhandle's first thought was that Posmo had betrayed him to the authorities. It *was* Posmo. Panhandle recognized the Mexican's pinto horse.

Enraged by what he thought was a trap, and with drunken contempt for the man he had cheated, Panhandle jerked out his gun and fired at the Mexican; fired again at the bulky figure behind Posmo, and staggered back as a slug shattered his shoulder. Cursing, he swung round and emptied his gun into the blur of riders that separated and spread across the street, returning his fire from the vantage of the shadows. Flinging his empty gun at the nearest rider, Panhandle lurched toward the doorway where Cheyenne and Bartley stood watching. He had almost made the curb when he lunged and fell. He rose and tried to crawl to the shelter of the doorway. One of Sneed's men spurred forward and shot Panhandle in the back. He sank down, his body twitching.

Bartley gasped as he saw the rider deliberately throw another shot into the dying man. Then Cheyenne's arm jerked up. The rider swerved and pitched from the saddle. Another of

Sneed's men crossed the patch of light, and a splinter ripped from the door-casing where Cheyenne stood. Cheyenne's gun came down again and the rider pitched forward and fell. His horse galloped down the street. Again Cheyenne fired, and again. Then, in the sudden stillness that followed, Cheyenne stepped out and dragged Panhandle into the hallway. Some one shouted. A window above the saloon opposite was raised. Doors opened and men came out, questioning each other, gathering in a group in front of the Hole-in-the-Wall.

Stunned by the sudden shock of events, the snakelike flash of guns in the semi-darkness, and the realization that several men had been gravely wounded, perhaps killed, Bartley heard Cheyenne's voice as though from a distance.

Cheyenne's hand was on Bartley's arm. "Come on. The game is closed for the night."

As they stepped from the doorway a man stopped them and asked what had happened.

"We're goin' for a doctor," said Cheyenne. "Somebody got hurt."

Hastening along the shadowy wall of the building, they turned a corner and by a roundabout way reached the city marshal's office.

The marshal, who had been summoned in haste, was at his desk. "Sneed and his bunch got Panhandle," stated Cheyenne quietly. "Mr. Bartley, here, saw the row. Four of Sneed's men are down. One got away."

"Sure it was Sneed?"

"I reckon your men will fetch him in, right soon. Panhandle

got Sneed and a Mexican, before they stopped him."

Colonel Stevenson glanced at Cheyenne's belt and holster. Cheyenne drew his gun and handed it to the marshal. "She's fresh loaded," he said.

"Cheyenne emptied his gun trying to fight off the men who killed Panhandle," said Bartley, stepping forward.

"And you're sure they were Sneed's men?" queried the marshal.

Cheyenne nodded.

"I am obliged to you," said the marshal. "But I'll have to detain you both until after the inquest."

CHAPTER XXV

TWO TRAILS HOME

Bartley was the chief witness at the inquest. He told his story in a manner that impressed the coroner's jury. Senator Brown was present, and identified one of the dead outlaws as Sneed. Posmo, killed by Panhandle's first shot, was known in Phoenix. Panhandle, riddled with bullets, was also identified by the Senator, Cheyenne, and several habitues of the gambling-hall. Bartley himself identified the body of one man as that of Hull.

Cheyenne was the last witness called. He admitted that he had had trouble with Panhandle Sears, and that he was looking for him when the fight started; that Sneed and his men had unexpectedly taken the quarrel out of his hands, and that he had fired exactly five shots at the men who had killed Panhandle and it had been close work, and easy. Panhandle had put up a game fight. The odds had been heavily against him. He had been standing in the light of the gambling-hall doorway while the men who had killed him had been in the shadow. "He didn't have a chance," concluded Cheyenne.

"You say you were looking for this man Sears, and yet you took his part against Sneed's outfit?" queried the coroner.

"I didn't just say so. Mr. Bartley said that."

"Mr. Bartley seems to be the only disinterested witness of the shooting," observed the coroner.

"If there is any further evidence needed to convince the jury that Mr. Bartley's statements are impartial and correct, you might read this," declared the city marshal. "It is the antemortem statement of one of Sneed's men, taken at the hospital at three-fifteen this morning. He died at four o'clock."

The coroner read the statement aloud. Ten minutes later the verdict was given. The deceased, named severally, had met death by gunshot wounds, *at the hands of parties unknown.*

It was a caustic verdict, intended for the benefit of the cattle- and horse-thieves of the Southwest. It conveyed the hint that the city of Phoenix was prompt to resent the presence of such gentry within its boundaries. One of the daily papers commented upon the fact that "the parties unknown" must have been fast and efficient gunmen. Cheyenne's name was not mentioned, and that was due to the influence of the marshal, Senator Brown, and the mayor, which left readers of the papers to infer that the police of Phoenix had handled the matter themselves.

Through the evidence of the outlaw who had survived long enough to make a statement, the Box-S horses were traced to a ranch in the neighborhood of Tucson, identified, and finally returned to their owner.

The day following the inquest, Bartley and Cheyenne left Phoenix, with Fort Apache as their first tentative destination, and with the promise of much rugged and wonderful country in between as an incentive to journey again with his companion, although Bartley needed no special incentive. At close range Bartley had beheld the killing of several men. And he could not free himself from the vision of Panhandle crawling toward him in the patch of white light, the flitting of horsemen back and forth, and the red flash of six-guns. Bartley was only too anxious to leave the place.

It was not until they were two days out of Phoenix that Cheyenne mentioned the fight—and then he did so casually, as though seeking an opinion from his comrade.

Bartley merely said he was glad Cheyenne had not killed Panhandle. Cheyenne pondered a while, riding loosely, and gazing down at the trail.

"I reckon I would 'a' killed him—if I'd 'a' got the chance," he said. "I meant to. No, it wasn't me or Panhandle that settled that argument: it was somethin' bigger than us. Folks that reads about the fight, knowin' I was in Phoenix, will most like say that I got him. Let 'em say so. I know I didn't; and you know I didn't—and that's good enough for me."

"And Dorothy and Aunt Jane and Little Jim," said Bartley.

"Meanin' Little Jim won't have to grow up knowin' that his father was a killer."

"I was thinking of that."

"Well, right here is where I quit thinkin' about it and talkin' about it. If that dog of yours there was to kill a coyote, in a fair fight, I reckon he wouldn't think about it long."

A few minutes later Cheyenne spoke of the country they were in.

"She's rough and unfriendly, right here," he said. "But north a ways she sure makes up for it. There's big spruce and high mesas and grass to your pony's knees and water 'most anywhere you look for it. I ain't much on huntin'. But there's plenty deer and wild turkey up that way, and some bear. And with a bent pin and a piece of string a fella can catch all the trout he wants. Arizona is a mighty surprisin' State, in spots. Most folks from the East think she's sagebrush and sand, except the Grand Canon; but that's kind of rented out to tourists, most of the time. I like the Painted Desert better."

"Where haven't you been?" said Bartley, laughing.

"Well, I ain't been North for quite a spell."

And Cheyenne fell silent, thinking of Laramie, of the broad prairies of Wyoming, of his old homestead, and the days when he was happy with his wife and Little Jim. But he was not silent long. He visioned a plan that he might work out, after he had seen Aunt Jane and Uncle Frank again. Meanwhile, the sun was shining, the road wound among the ragged hills, and Filaree and Joshua stepped along briskly, their hoof-beats suggesting the rhythm of a song.

That night they camped in the hill country not far from a crossroads store. In the morning they bought a few provisions and an extra canteen.

"There's a piece of country between here and the real hills that is like to be dry," explained Cheyenne. "We're leavin' the road, this mornin', and cuttin' north. She's some rough, the way we're headed, but you'll like it."

From the sagebrush of the southern slopes they climbed slowly up to a country of scattered juniper. By noon they were among the pinons, following a dim bridle trail that Cheyenne's horses seemed to know.

"In a couple of days, I aim to spring a surprise on you," said Cheyenne as they turned in that night. "I figure to show you somethin' you been wantin' to see."

"Bring on your bears," said Bartley, laughing.

Cheyenne's moodiness had vanished. Frequently he hummed his old trail song as they rode. Next day, as they nooned among the spruce of the high country, Cheyenne suddenly drew the dice from his pocket and, turning them in his hands, finally tossed them over the rim-rock of the canon edging their camp. "It's a fool game," he said. And Bartley knew, by the otter's tone, that he did not alone refer to the game of dice.

The air was thin, clear, and vital with a quality that the air of the lower country lacked. Bartley felt an ambition to settle down and go to writing. He thought that he now had material enough and to spare. They were in a country, vast, fenceless, verdant—almost awesome in its timbered silences. His imagination was stirred.

From their noon camp they rode into the timber and from the timber into a mountain meadow, knee-deep with lush grass. There was no visible trail across the meadow but the horses seemed to know which way to go. After crossing the meadow, Filaree, leading the cavalcade, turned and took a steep trail down the side of a hidden canon, a mighty chasm, rock-walled and somber. At the bottom the horses drank, and, crossing the stream, climbed the farther side. In an hour they were again on the rim, plodding noiselessly through the sun-flecked shadows of the giant spruce.

"How about that surprise?" queried Bartley.

"Ain't this good enough?" said Cheyenne, gesturing roundabout.

"Gosh, yes! Lead on, Macduff."

About four that afternoon the horses pricked their ears and quickened their pace. Filaree and Joshua especially seemed interested in getting along the silent trail; and presently the trail merged with another trail, more defined. A few hundred yards down this trail, and Bartley saw a big log cabin; to the left and beyond it a corral, empty, and with the bars down. Bartley had never seen the place before, and did not realize where he was, yet he had noticed that the horses seemed to know the place.

"We won't stop by," said Cheyenne.

"Any one live there?"

"Sneed used to," stated Cheyenne.

Then Bartley knew that they were not far from the San Andreas Valley and—well, the Lawrence ranch.

They dropped down a long trail into another canon which finally spread to a green valley dotted with ranches. The horses stepped briskly. Presently, rounding a bend, they saw a ranch-house, far below, and sharply defined squares of alfalfa.

"That house with the red roof—" said Bartley.

"That's her," asserted Cheyenne, a trifle ambiguously.

"Then we've swung round in a circle."

"We done crossed the res'avation, pardner. And we didn't see a dog-gone Injun."

Little Jim was the first to catch sight of them as they jogged down the last stretch of trail leaving the foothills. He recognized the horses long before their riders were near enough to be identified as his father and Bartley.

Little Jim did not rush to Aunt Jane and tell her excitedly that they were coming. Instead, he quietly saddled up his pony and rode out to meet them. Part-way up the slope he waited.

His greeting was not effusive. "I just thought I'd ride up and tell you folks that—'that I seen you comin'."

"How goes the hunting?" queried Bartley.

"Fine! I got six rabbits yesterday. Dorry is gittin' so she can shoot pretty good, too. How you makin' it, dad?"

Cheyenne pushed back his hat and gazed at his young son. "Pretty fair, for an old man," said Cheyenne presently. "You been behavin' yourself?"

"Sure."

"How would you like to ride a real hoss, once?"

"You mean *your* hoss?"

"Uh-huh."

"I'll trade you, even."

"No, you won't, son. But you can ride him down to the ranch, if you like."

Little Jim almost tumbled from his pony in his eagerness to

ride Joshua, his father's horse, with the big saddle and rope and the carbine under the stirrup leather.

"You musta made a long ride," declared Jimmy, as he scrambled up on Joshua. "Josh's shoes is worn thin. He'll be throwin' one, next."

Jimmy called attention to the horse's shoes, that his father and Bartley might not see how really pleased he was to ride a "real horse."

"Yes, a long ride. How is Aunt Jane and Dorry?"

"Oh, they're all right. Uncle Frank he cut twenty-two tons of alfalfa off the lower field last week."

Cheyenne sat sideways on Jimmy's pony as they rode down the last easy slope and turned into the ranch gate. Aunt Jane, who was busy cooking,—it seemed that Aunt Jane was always busy cooking something or other, when she wasn't dressmaking or mending clothing or ironing,—greeted them warmly. Frank was working down at the lower end. Dorry had gone to San Andreas. She would be back 'most any time, now. And weren't they hungry?

They were. And there was fresh milk and pie. But they put up the horses first.

Later, Cheyenne and Little Jim decided to walk down to the lower end of the ranch and see Uncle Frank. Cheyenne had washed his hands and face before eating, as had Bartley. But Bartley did not let it go at that. He begged some hot water and again washed and shaved, brushed his clothes, and changed his flannel shirt for a clean one. Then he strolled to the kitchen and chatted with Aunt Jane, who had read of the killing of the outlaws in Phoenix, and had many questions to ask. It had been a terrible tragedy. And Mr. Bartley had actually seen the shooting?

Aunt Jane was glad that Cheyenne had not been mixed up in it, especially as that man Sears had been killed. But now that he had been killed, people would talk less about her brother. It really had seemed an act of Providence that Cheyenne had had nothing to do with the shooting. Of course, Mr. Bartley knew about the trouble that her brother had had—and why he had never settled down—

"His name was not mentioned in the papers," said Bartley, thinking that he must say something.

"There's Dorry, now," said Aunt Jane, glancing through the kitchen window.

Bartley promptly excused himself and stepped out to the gate, which he vaulted and opened as Dorothy waved a greeting. Bartley carried the groceries in, and later helped unhitch the team. They chatted casually neither referring to the subject uppermost in their minds.

When Cheyenne returned, riding on a load of alfalfa with Uncle Frank and Little Jim, Bartley managed to let Uncle Frank know that he was not supposed to have had a hand in the Phoenix affair. Cheyenne thanked him.

"But you ain't talked with Dorry, yet, have you?" queried Cheyenne.

Bartley shook his head.

"She'll find out," stated Cheyenne. "You can't fool Dorry."

That evening, while Uncle Frank and Cheyenne were

discussing a matter which seemed confidential to themselves, and while Aunt Jane was quietly keeping an eye on Jimmy, who could hardly keep from interrupting his seniors—Bartley and Dorry didn't count, just then, for *they* were also talking together—Dorothy intimated to Bartley that she would like to talk with him alone. She did not say so, nor make any gesture to indicate her wish, yet Bartley interpreted her expression correctly.

He suggested that they step out to the veranda, where it was cooler. From the veranda they strolled to the big gate, and there she asked him, point-blank, to tell her just what had happened in Phoenix. She had read the papers, and she surmised that there was more to the affair than the papers printed. For instance, Senator Brown, upon his return to the Box-S, had kindly sent word to Aunt Jane that Cheyenne was all right. Bartley thought that the thoughtful Senator had rather spilled the beans.

"Did Cheyenne—" and Dorothy hesitated.

"Cheyenne didn't kill Sears," stated Bartley.

"You talked with Cheyenne, and got him to keep out of it?"

"I tried to. He wouldn't listen. Then I wished him good luck and told him I hoped he'd win."

Dorothy was puzzled. "How do you know he didn't?"

"Because I was standing beside him when it happened. I don't see why you shouldn't know about it. Cheyenne and I were just about to cross the street, that night, when we saw Panhandle coming down the opposite side. Sneed and his men, who were evidently waiting for him, called to Panhandle. Panhandle must have thought it was the sheriff, or the city marshal. It happened suddenly. Panhandle began firing at Sneed and his riders. They shot him down just as he reached the curb in front of us. They kept on shooting at him as he lay in the street. Cheyenne couldn't stand that. He emptied his gun, trying to keep them off—and he emptied some saddles."

"Thank you for trying to—to give Cheyenne my message," said Dorothy. And she shook hands with him.

"Do you know this is the loveliest vista I have seen since leaving Phoenix—this San Andreas Valley," said Bartley.

"But you came through the Apache Forest," said Dorothy, not for the sake of argument, but because Bartley was still holding her hand.

"Yes. But you don't happen to live in the Apache Forest."

"But, Mr. Bartley—"

"John, please."

"Cheyenne calls you Jack."

"Better still. Do you think Aunt Jane would mind if we walked up the road as far as—well, as far as the spring?"

"Hadn't you better ask her?"

"No. But she wouldn't object. Would you?"

Slowly Dorothy withdrew her hand and Bartley opened the big gate. As they walked down the dim, starlit road they were startled by the advent of a yellow dog that bounded from the brush and whined joyously.

"And I had forgotten him," said Bartley. "Oh, he's mine! I can't get away from the fact. He adopted me, and has followed me clear through. I had forgotten that he is afraid to come into a ranch. And I am ashamed to say that I forgot to feed him, to-night. He isn't at all beautiful, but he's tremendously loyal."

"And he shall have a good supper when we get back," declared Dorothy.

The yellow dog padded along behind them in the dusk, content to be with his master again. Bartley talked with Dorothy about his plans, his hopes, and her promise to become the heroine of his new story. Then he surprised her by stating that he had decided to make a home in the San Andreas Valley.

"You really don't know anything about me, or my people," he said. "And I want you to know. My only living relative is my sister, and she is scandalously well-to-do. Her husband makes money manufacturing hooks and eyes. He's not romantic, but he's solid. As for me—"

And Bartley spoke of his own income, just what he could afford to spend each month, and just how much he managed to save, and his ambition to earn more. Dorothy realized that he was talking to her just as he would have talked to a chum—a man friend, without reserve, and she liked him for it. She had been curious about him, his vocation, and even about his plans; and she felt a glow of affection because he had seemed so loyal to his friendship with Cheyenne, and because he had been kind to Little Jim Hastings. While doing so with no other thought than to please the boy, Bartley had made no mistake in buying him that new rifle.

As they came to the big rock by the roadside—a spot which

Bartley had good reason to remember—he paused and glanced at Dorothy. She was laughing.

"You looked so funny that day. You were the most dilapidated-looking person—for a writer—"

"I imagine I was, after Hull got through with me. Let's sit down awhile. I want to tell you what I should like to do. Are you comfortable?"

Dorothy nodded.

"Well," said Bartley, seating himself beside her, "I should like to rent a small place in the valley, a place just big enough for two, and then settle down and write this story. Then, if I sold it, I think I should lock up, get a pack-horse and another saddle-horse, outfit for a long trip, and then take the trail north and travel for, say, six months, seeing the country, camping along the way, visiting with folks, and incidentally gathering material for another story. It could be done."

"But why rent a place, if you plan to leave it right away?"

"Because I should want a home to come to, a place to think of when I was on the trails. You know a fellow can't wander up and down the world forever. I like to travel, but I think a chap ought to spend at least half a year under a roof. Don't you?"

"I was thinking of Cheyenne," said Dorothy musingly.

"I think of him a great deal," declared Bartley.

Dorothy glanced up at him from her pondering.

Henry Herbert Knibbs

Bartley leaned toward her. "Dorothy, will you help me make that home, here in the valley, and be my comrade on the trails?"

"Hadn't you better ask Aunt Jane?" said Dorothy softly, yet with a touch of humor.

"Do you mean it?" Bartley's voice was boyishly enthusiastic, like the voice of a chum, a hearty comrade. "But how about your own folks?"

Dorothy's answer was not given then and there, in words. Nor yet by gesture, nor in any visible way—there being no moon that early in the evening. After a brief interval—or, at least, it seemed brief—they rose and strolled back down the road, the yellow dog padding faithfully at their heels. Presently—

"Hey, Dorry!" came in a shrill voice.

"It's the scout!" exclaimed Bartley, laughing.

"We're coming, Jimmy," called Dorothy.

"But before we're taken into custody—" said Bartley; and as mentioned before, the moon had not appeared.

Little Jim, astride of the ranch gate, querulously demanded where they had been and why they had not told him they were going somewhere.

"And you left the gate open, and—everything!" concluded Jimmy.

"We just went for a walk," said Dorothy.

"What's the use of walkin' up the old road in the dark?" queried Jimmy. "You can't see anything."

"What do you say to a rabbit hunt to-morrow morning early?" asked Bartley.

"Nope!" declared Little Jim decisively. "'Cause my dad was talkin' with Aunt Jane and Uncle Frank, and dad says me and him are goin' back to Laramie where ma is. And we're goin' on the *train*. Aunt Jane she cried. But shucks! We ain't goin' to stay in Laramie all the time. Dad says if things rib up right, me and ma and him are comin' back to live in the valley. Don't you wish you was goin', Dorry?"

"You run along and tell Aunt Jane we're coming," said Bartley.

Little Jim hesitated. But then, Mr. Bartley had bought him that new rifle. Jimmy pattered down the path to the lighted doorway, delivered his message, and pattered back again toward the gate, wasting no time *en route*. Halfway to the gate he stopped. Mr. Bartley was standing very close to Dorry—in fact, Jimmy was amazed to see him kiss her. Jimmy turned and trotted back to the house.

"Shucks!" he exclaimed. "I thought he liked guns and things more'n girls!"

But Jimmy was too loyal to tell what he had seen. After all, Dorry was mighty fine, for a girl. She could ride and shoot, and she never told on him when he had done wrong.

With a skip and a hop Jimmy burst into the room. "We're goin' on the *train*," he declared. "Ain't we, dad?"

Dorothy and Bartley came in. Bartley glanced at Cheyenne,

hesitated, and then thrust out his hand.

"Good luck to your new venture," he said heartily.

"Same to you, pardner!" And Cheyenne included Dorry in his glance.

"I want to ask Aunt Jane's advice," stated Bartley.

"Then," said Cheyenne, "I reckon me and Frank and Jimmy'll step out and take a look at the stars. She's a wonderful night."

Choose from Thousands of 1stWorldLibrary Classics By

A. M. Barnard
Ada Leverson
Adolphus William Ward
Aesop
Agatha Christie
Alexander Aaronsohn
Alexander Kielland
Alexandre Dumas
Alfred Gatty
Alfred Ollivant
Alice Duer Miller
Alice Turner Curtis
Alice Dunbar
Allen Chapman
Alleyne Ireland
Ambrose Bierce
Amelia E. Barr
Amory H. Bradford
Andrew Lang
Andrew McFarland Davis
Andy Adams
Angela Brazil
Anna Alice Chapin
Anna Sewell
Annie Besant
Annie Hamilton Donnell
Annie Payson Call
Annie Roe Carr
Annonaymous
Anton Chekhov
Archibald Lee Fletcher
Arnold Bennett
Arthur C. Benson
Arthur Conan Doyle
Arthur M. Winfield
Arthur Ransome
Arthur Schnitzler
Arthur Train
Atticus
B.H. Baden-Powell
B. M. Bower
B. C. Chatterjee
Baroness Emmuska Orczy
Baroness Orczy
Basil King
Bayard Taylor
Ben Macomber
Bertha Muzzy Bower
Bjornstjerne Bjornson

Booth Tarkington
Boyd Cable
Bram Stoker
C. Collodi
C. E. Orr
C. M. Ingleby
Carolyn Wells
Catherine Parr Traill
Charles A. Eastman
Charles Amory Beach
Charles Dickens
Charles Dudley Warner
Charles Farrar Browne
Charles Ives
Charles Kingsley
Charles Klein
Charles Hanson Towne
Charles Lathrop Pack
Charles Romyn Dake
Charles Whibley
Charles Willing Beale
Charlotte M. Braeme
Charlotte M. Yonge
Charlotte Perkins Stetson
Clair W. Hayes
Clarence Day Jr.
Clarence E. Mulford
Clemence Housman
Confucius
Coningsby Dawson
Cornelis DeWitt Wilcox
Cyril Burleigh
D. H. Lawrence
Daniel Defoe
David Garnett
Dinah Craik
Don Carlos Janes
Donald Keyhoe
Dorothy Kilner
Dougan Clark
Douglas Fairbanks
E. Nesbit
E. P. Roe
E. Phillips Oppenheim
E. S. Brooks
Earl Barnes
Edgar Rice Burroughs
Edith Van Dyne
Edith Wharton

Edward Everett Hale
Edward J. O'Biren
Edward S. Ellis
Edwin L. Arnold
Eleanor Atkins
Eleanor Hallowell Abbott
Eliot Gregory
Elizabeth Gaskell
Elizabeth McCracken
Elizabeth Von Arnim
Ellem Key
Emerson Hough
Emilie F. Carlen
Emily Bronte
Emily Dickinson
Enid Bagnold
Enilor Macartney Lane
Erasmus W. Jones
Ernie Howard Pie
Ethel May Dell
Ethel Turner
Ethel Watts Mumford
Eugene Sue
Eugenie Foa
Eugene Wood
Eustace Hale Ball
Evelyn Everett-green
Everard Cotes
F. H. Cheley
F. J. Cross
F. Marion Crawford
Fannie E. Newberry
Federick Austin Ogg
Ferdinand Ossendowski
Fergus Hume
Florence A. Kilpatrick
Fremont B. Deering
Francis Bacon
Francis Darwin
Frances Hodgson Burnett
Frances Parkinson Keyes
Frank Gee Patchin
Frank Harris
Frank Jewett Mather
Frank L. Packard
Frank V. Webster
Frederic Stewart Isham
Frederick Trevor Hill
Frederick Winslow Taylor

Friedrich Kerst
Friedrich Nietzsche
Fyodor Dostoyevsky
G.A. Henty
G.K. Chesterton
Gabrielle E. Jackson
Garrett P. Serviss
Gaston Leroux
George A. Warren
George Ade
Geroge Bernard Shaw
George Cary Eggleston
George Durston
George Ebers
George Eliot
George Gissing
George MacDonald
George Meredith
George Orwell
George Sylvester Viereck
George Tucker
George W. Cable
George Wharton James
Gertrude Atherton
Gordon Casserly
Grace E. King
Grace Gallatin
Grace Greenwood
Grant Allen
Guillermo A. Sherwell
Gulielma Zollinger
Gustav Flaubert
H. A. Cody
H. B. Irving
H.C. Bailey
H. G. Wells
H. H. Munro
H. Irving Hancock
H. R. Naylor
H. Rider Haggard
H. W. C. Davis
Haldeman Julius
Hall Caine
Hamilton Wright Mabie
Hans Christian Andersen
Harold Avery
Harold McGrath
Harriet Beecher Stowe
Harry Castlemon
Harry Coghill
Harry Houidini

Hayden Carruth
Helent Hunt Jackson
Helen Nicolay
Hendrik Conscience
Hendy David Thoreau
Henri Barbusse
Henrik Ibsen
Henry Adams
Henry Ford
Henry Frost
Henry James
Henry Jones Ford
Henry Seton Merriman
Henry W Longfellow
Herbert A. Giles
Herbert Carter
Herbert N. Casson
Herman Hesse
Hildegard G. Frey
Homer
Honore De Balzac
Horace B. Day
Horace Walpole
Horatio Alger Jr.
Howard Pyle
Howard R. Garis
Hugh Lofting
Hugh Walpole
Humphry Ward
Ian Maclaren
Inez Haynes Gillmore
Irving Bacheller
Isabel Cecilia Williams
Isabel Hornibrook
Israel Abrahams
Ivan Turgenev
J.G.Austin
J. Henri Fabre
J. M. Barrie
J. M. Walsh
J. Macdonald Oxley
J. R. Miller
J. S. Fletcher
J. S. Knowles
J. Storer Clouston
J. W. Duffield
Jack London
Jacob Abbott
James Allen
James Andrews
James Baldwin

James Branch Cabell
James DeMille
James Joyce
James Lane Allen
James Lane Allen
James Oliver Curwood
James Oppenheim
James Otis
James R. Driscoll
Jane Abbott
Jane Austen
Jane L. Stewart
Janet Aldridge
Jens Peter Jacobsen
Jerome K. Jerome
Jessie Graham Flower
John Buchan
John Burroughs
John Cournos
John F. Kennedy
John Gay
John Glasworthy
John Habberton
John Joy Bell
John Kendrick Bangs
John Milton
John Philip Sousa
John Taintor Foote
Jonas Lauritz Idemil Lie
Jonathan Swift
Joseph A. Altsheler
Joseph Carey
Joseph Conrad
Joseph E. Badger Jr
Joseph Hergesheimer
Joseph Jacobs
Jules Vernes
Julian Hawthrone
Julie A Lippmann
Justin Huntly McCarthy
Kakuzo Okakura
Karle Wilson Baker
Kate Chopin
Kenneth Grahame
Kenneth McGaffey
Kate Langley Bosher
Kate Langley Bosher
Katherine Cecil Thurston
Katherine Stokes
L. A. Abbot
L. T. Meade

L. Frank Baum
Latta Griswold
Laura Dent Crane
Laura Lee Hope
Laurence Housman
Lawrence Beasley
Leo Tolstoy
Leonid Andreyev
Lewis Carroll
Lewis Sperry Chafer
Lilian Bell
Lloyd Osbourne
Louis Hughes
Louis Joseph Vance
Louis Tracy
Louisa May Alcott
Lucy Fitch Perkins
Lucy Maud Montgomery
Luther Benson
Lydia Miller Middleton
Lyndon Orr
M. Corvus
M. H. Adams
Margaret E. Sangster
Margret Howth
Margaret Vandercook
Margaret W. Hungerford
Margret Penrose
Maria Edgeworth
Maria Thompson Daviess
Mariano Azuela
Marion Polk Angellotti
Mark Overton
Mark Twain
Mary Austin
Mary Catherine Crowley
Mary Cole
Mary Hastings Bradley
Mary Roberts Rinehart
Mary Rowlandson
M. Wollstonecraft Shelley
Maud Lindsay
Max Beerbohm
Myra Kelly
Nathaniel Hawthrone
Nicolo Machiavelli
O. F. Walton
Oscar Wilde

Owen Johnson
P.G. Wodehouse
Paul and Mabel Thorne
Paul G. Tomlinson
Paul Severing
Percy Brebner
Percy Keese Fitzhugh
Peter B. Kyne
Plato
Quincy Allen
R. Derby Holmes
R. L. Stevenson
R. S. Ball
Rabindranath Tagore
Rahul Alvares
Ralph Bonehill
Ralph Henry Barbour
Ralph Victor
Ralph Waldo Emmerson
Rene Descartes
Ray Cummings
Rex Beach
Rex E. Beach
Richard Harding Davis
Richard Jefferies
Richard Le Gallienne
Robert Barr
Robert Frost
Robert Gordon Anderson
Robert L. Drake
Robert Lansing
Robert Lynd
Robert Michael Ballantyne
Robert W. Chambers
Rosa Nouchette Carey
Rudyard Kipling
Saint Augustine
Samuel B. Allison
Samuel Hopkins Adams
Sarah Bernhardt
Sarah C. Hallowell
Selma Lagerlof
Sherwood Anderson
Sigmund Freud
Standish O'Grady
Stanley Weyman
Stella Benson
Stella M. Francis

Stephen Crane
Stewart Edward White
Stijn Streuvels
Swami Abhedananda
Swami Parmananda
T. S. Ackland
T. S. Arthur
The Princess Der Ling
Thomas A. Janvier
Thomas A Kempis
Thomas Anderton
Thomas Bailey Aldrich
Thomas Bulfinch
Thomas De Quincey
Thomas Dixon
Thomas H. Huxley
Thomas Hardy
Thomas More
Thornton W. Burgess
U. S. Grant
Upton Sinclair
Valentine Williams
Various Authors
Vaughan Kester
Victor Appleton
Victor G. Durham
Victoria Cross
Virginia Woolf
Wadsworth Camp
Walter Camp
Walter Scott
Washington Irving
Wilbur Lawton
Wilkie Collins
Willa Cather
Willard F. Baker
William Dean Howells
William le Queux
W. Makepeace Thackeray
William W. Walter
William Shakespeare
Winston Churchill
Yei Theodora Ozaki
Yogi Ramacharaka
Young E. Allison
Zane Grey